ITALY REVEALED

ITALY

REVEALED

Charles FitzRoy

—— WITH PHOTOGRAPHY BY ——

Joe Cornish

LITTLE, BROWN AND COMPANY
BOSTON · NEW YORK · TORONTO · LONDON

Text copyright © 1994 by Charles FitzRoy
Photographs copyright © 1994 by Joe Cornish
Map copyright © 1994 by Anthony Sidwell

First Edition

ISBN 0-316-28442-4

Library of Congress Catalog Card Number 94-76028
A CIP catalogue record for this book is available from the British Library

Designed by Andrew Barron and Collis Clements Associates
Typeset by SX Composing Ltd., Rayleigh, Essex

Published simultaneously in the United States of America by
Little, Brown and Company (Inc.),
in Great Britain by Little, Brown and Company (UK) Ltd,
and in Canada by Little, Brown & Company (Canada) Limited

PRINTED AND BOUND IN ITALY

Half title: The Cappella di Piazza is a handsome commemoration
of Siena's delivery from the Black Death in 1348. It forms the
entrance loggia to the Palazzo Pubblico.

This page: The evocative medieval towers of San Gimignano rise
above the dawn mist.

CONTENTS

INTRODUCTION

T his book aims at all those who have ever sampled the myriad charms of Italy, or have felt the urge to do so. Whether it be the marvellous works of art, the beauty of the landscape, the pleasures of eating and drinking, or the Italians themselves, with their quick wit and intelligence, there is something in this enchanting country to appeal to every kind of visitor.

I have tried to encompass the astonishing diversity of works of art spread throughout Italy. In antiquity, I have by-passed Rome and Naples in favour of the lesser-known Roman site of Aquileia, the Etruscan towns on the border of Tuscany and Lazio, and the Greek temples and Roman mosaics of Sicily. Medieval Italy is encapsulated by the Romanesque and Gothic abbeys and monasteries of Tuscany and Umbria, the Norman cathedrals of Sicily, and the intricate fortified towns of the Veneto.

Previous pages, main
picture: A panoramic view of
the Orcia valley south of
Siena seen from the ancient
Roman Via Cassia.
Detail: The columns of the
Greek Temple of Herakles at
Agrigento stand out against
the deep blue sky.

Italian Renaissance art is one of the supreme achievements of European civilization. I have concentrated on the most cultivated patrons of the arts, on the fresco cycles artists painted in their native provinces, and on the villas and gardens which still stand untouched in the countryside. I end with the baroque, a last outpouring of the Italian artistic genius, ranging from the model town of Noto and the inventive sculpture of Serpotta, to the formal gardens surrounding Lucca and the exuberant frescoes of Tiepolo.

I have avoided the main tourist centres. Rather than dealing with Florence, Venice or Rome, where you are liable to be buried beneath the sheer weight of mass tourism, I have chosen to concentrate on works of art which still stand in their original settings. The rich Italian landscape provides endless variety, from the backbone of the Apennines to the well-watered plains of the north, the rolling hills of Tuscany and Umbria, and the dramatic volcanic mountains of Sicily.

The itineraries in this book are designed for the motorist who has no inclination to suffer the full terror of confronting Italian drivers en masse in the narrow streets of a city (where the definition of a split second is the time that it takes a driver to hoot his horn when the traffic lights turn green). It is in the countryside that you can best capture the unchanging face of Italy.

This is perhaps best seen in the village festivals which hark back for centuries, whether it is a theatrical evening in the green theatre at Marlia, a cheese-rolling competition in the piazza at Pienza, or a medieval archery contest in the fields outside San Sepolcro. The Italians invented Carnival and the *commedia dell'arte*, and developed the art of fireworks and torchlight processions, and there is nowhere better to watch a spectacle. I once bumped into an Easter procession in the mountains behind Mount Etna. Jesus, his halo slipping from his head, was sharing a joke with a Roman legionary, while Mary Magdalene gracefully accepted a glass of wine from a bystander.

Following a route off the beaten track is an ideal way of sampling the joys of Italian cuisine where home-made pasta in a small trattoria is often far tastier than the better-known dishes which appear on the menu turistico. Each region prides itself on its cooking, a legacy of centuries of independence. Even in antiquity the Etruscans were covering the walls of their tombs with paintings of banquets and revellers. Never breathe it to a Frenchman, but many of their finest dishes, including sorbets, date back to the Tuscan cooks Catherine de' Medici took in her entourage when she left Italy to marry Henry II in 1535.

Sightseeing is more relaxing away from the large cities. The Italians themselves appear at their best, displaying the spontaneous charm which has so enthralled generations of visitors to the country. There is less pressure to see all the main sites, which invariably leads to cultural saturation. By following a thematic itinerary, you can gain an insight into a subject, and your sensations are likely to be fresher as you pursue a particular artist and study the success with which he overcomes the problems that confront him.

ITALY

Mediterranean Sea

SICILY

MILAN

The VENETO & FRIULI
tours 8~12

Udine

Treviso

Vicenza

Padua

Venice

UMBRIA & The MARCHE
tours 13~16

Prato

Lucca

Pisa

Florence

Arezzo

Siena

Urbino

Assisi

Perugia

Ascoli Piceno

Spoleto

TUSCANY &
NORTHERN LAZIO
tours 1~7

Palermo

Taormina

SICILY
tours 17~21

Agrigento

Syracuse

ROME

Mediterranean Sea

TUSCANY AND
NORTHERN LAZIO

The romance of Tuscany's dramatic history, from medieval legends to Renaissance princes, visible in the towers bristling from every hill-town, and the olive groves and vineyards covering the landscape, encapsulates the charm of Italy. The countryside is filled with unchanging images: a pair of white oxen tilling the red earth, a bell tolling from a medieval campanile, and the pungent scent of cypress and box on a hot summer's afternoon. The trappings of modernism merge with the past: flashlights pop as a couple exchange marriage vows beneath a Quattrocento fresco, and every Sienese believes in the horse running in the colours of his *contrada* (parish) in the Palio as though his life depended on it.

This is all totally natural to a Tuscan. He is never

13

pretentious, and even the most successful businessman, briefcase in hand, will cross a busy street to placate an irate *bambino*. Tuscan cooking reflects this simplicity. Its ingredients are always fresh, and based on the products of the countryside, the vegetables, olives and game visible in every field. This is where you are most likely to see freshly made pasta laid out on the counter of a small trattoria as it has been for centuries.

The extraordinary depth of Tuscan culture allows even the most ardent sightseer the chance to make a new discovery. This is, sadly, no longer true of Florence, the city of Giotto, Dante and Michelangelo, with its priceless collections bequeathed by the Medici, and the first stop on the tourist menu. Many people soon tire of shuffling in queues round stifling museums. Far better to concentrate on the other cities in Tuscany, in particular Siena and Lucca. Siena is a medieval jewel, whose central piazza, the Campo, set at the junction of its three hills, is one of the most exquisite pieces of town planning in all Italy. Lucca has preserved its atmosphere of faded charm, undisturbed by the hordes inundating neighbouring Pisa. Most of the tours in this section can be covered from one of these two cities.

Each of the main Tuscan cities is fiercely protective of its independence. A Sienese would rather die than admit he is a Florentine, and no sooner has a car with Florentine number plates parked in a side street than a policeman appears miraculously to give it a ticket. This harks back to ancient rivalries. Siena, like Lucca, Pisa and Arezzo, was a Ghibelline city (supporting the Emperor) while Florence was always Guelph (supporting the Pope). Each city had its patron saint: Siena was under the protection of the Virgin, Lucca had St Martin, and the Florentine armies charged into battle crying the name of San Giovanni. This helps to emphasize the individuality of each city, something which is much more apparent than in England or France, which were united much earlier.

I have tried to show the sheer variety of works of art in Tuscany and over the border in Lazio. Siena, with its Gothic palaces, heraldic emblems, and its celebration of the Palio is still steeped in its medieval past. The surrounding landscape abounds in ancient abbeys and monasteries. The Florentine countryside is filled with Renaissance works of art commissioned by the Medici, who were able to call on the services of the most talented collection of artists the world had seen since the age of Pericles in fifth-century Athens. Even in the provincial backwaters of Arezzo and Borgo Sansepolcro, Piero della Francesca painted a series of frescoes which rival the finest contemporary paintings in Florence. The Renaissance covered every field of art, and around Viterbo, Vignola designed a number of gardens which inspired the baroque gardeners around Lucca, and continue to influence garden designers to this day. And in the lonely Maremma the enigmatic Etruscans produced painting and sculpture which rival and even surpass the art of the ancient Romans.

The bulk of the tours cover the great age of the Renaissance, when a series of outstanding men changed our perception of the world. Founders of the banking system, innovators in biology, botany and zoology, experts in the study of history and political doctrines – there seemed no limit to the achievements of the Tuscan *uomo universale*. In literature, Dante single-handedly transformed the Tuscan dialect into the Italian language.

The leading artists were equally happy switching from one art to another. Giotto, with no architectural training, designed the campanile for the Duomo in Florence; Francesco di Giorgio was equally gifted as a sculptor, painter and architect; and Michelangelo surpassed all his contemporaries in his mastery of all the arts, even designing the fortifications for the defence of Florence during the siege of 1529-30. These artists were often inventive mathematicians and scientists. Brunelleschi, thwarted as a sculptor, turned to architecture and discovered the laws of perspective; the painter Uccello would sit up far into the night poring over his mathematical doodles, despite the pleading of his wife to come to bed; and ideas poured from the extraordinary mind of Leonardo da Vinci, including the design for a primitive flying machine.

The politicians were no less talented. Machiavelli's *The Prince* became the handbook for all aspiring rulers, and Lorenzo Il Magnifico composed some of the most delightful poetry of the entire Renaissance while ruling Florence. The fame of these brilliant men resounded throughout Europe. Their talents were eagerly sought by kings and princes, and wherever they went artists flocked to study their achievements.

Tuscany is full of her native sons' works of genius. I have avoided the well-trodden routes around the Uffizi and the Pitti Palace with their swarms of visitors, to concentrate on works of art in their original settings, churches and abbeys in remote landscapes, paintings in cloisters, and gardens carved out of the hillsides. Such is the wealth of art on offer that every village possesses something of beauty. Tuscany and northern Lazio are therefore ideally suited to the concept of the thematic itinerary, and in a leisurely day's sightseeing you can cover any one of the various tours.

The landscape is very varied, from the mountainous Apennines and the Apuan Alps in the north, to the Chianti hills between Florence and Siena, and the panoramic landscapes on either side of the Via Cassia south of Siena. To the east, towards the Umbrian border, the countryside is softer, while to the west the Maremma stretches down to the coast. Such variety has provided inspiration from the time of Petrarch and Dante onwards, and you can easily imagine, when travelling through southern Tuscany, with its distant views of Monte Amiata, Pope Pius II, a passionate lover of his native countryside, setting up court on the mountain in the summer of 1462, and receiving ambassadors beneath a chestnut tree or by a cool spring in a grove of olives.

RENAISSANCE GENIUS

MONTERCHI · BORGO SANSEPOLCRO · SAN FRANCESCO, AREZZO

Piero della Francesca's fresco of the pregnant Madonna hangs in a small chapel outside the village of Monterchi. It is one of the most poignant paintings of the Quattrocento.

Starting-point: Monterchi
Recommended time: A short day or half a day if the tour ends with Borgo Sansepolcro
Length of tour: 35 miles (55km)
Best time of year: April/May or October
Finishing-point:
San Francesco, Arezzo

The province of Arezzo remains a backwater. It has some pretty countryside along the Umbrian border, and some picturesque festivals, notably the Giostra del Saracino (a jousting tournament) in the Piazza Grande in Arezzo, and the archery contest between Borgo Sansepolcro and Gubbio, with the contestants dressed in medieval costume. Yet it is much neglected, except by aficionados of Piero della Francesca. An artist of genius, whose paintings were ignored for centuries, Piero is now appreciated for his true merit. Literature floods off the printing presses, his frescoes are cleaned and recleaned, exhibitions are mounted in his honour, and the *cognoscenti* flock to 'do the Piero trail'. Piero's greatest works are still situated in a small area in eastern Tuscany and the neighbouring town of Urbino just across the Apennines (see page 102). The three sites in Tuscany can easily be seen in a day, but, to avoid mental, let alone physical exhaustion, the Ducal Palace at Urbino should be left to a separate expedition.

Piero is an endlessly fascinating painter. His calm, monumental figures seem to speak to us across the centuries in a way that the works of few artists can rival. He was not prolific, and you are fortunate still to be able to see most of his best works in their original settings. We know very little about his life and character, or about his paintings. This has led to a battle royal between art historians, who differ wildly in their interpretation of the chronology and meaning of the various works and the participation of Piero's pupils. If you care to wade through the copious literature, especially on the 'Flagellation' in Urbino, this makes for richly comical reading, a professorial jousting match, with a novel theory no sooner set up on a pedestal than a new contender arrives in the lists to drive his quill through it.

What is indisputable is Piero's love of his native Tuscany. Although a well-travelled artist who studied under Domenico Veneziano in Florence, and who worked in Rome, and the courts of Ferrara, Rimini and Urbino, he felt most at home in and around his native Borgo Sansepolcro where he possibly worked under the Sienese Sassetta. This is most apparent in the fresco of the Madonna del Parto Piero painted for the wayside chapel of Santa Maria della Momentana outside the small borgo of Monterchi, his mother's home town. I have chosen this painting first because you need to visit it alone, which you are most likely to be able to do in the early morning, to capture its intimate atmosphere.

The small chapel in which the painting normally hangs stands off a dusty road rising up the hill behind Monterchi (at the moment of writing it has the misfortune to be honouring Piero's quincentenary by sitting in a restoration studio). The fresco possesses a disconcerting intimacy. Two angels draw back the curtains of a tent to reveal the pregnant Madonna, portrayed as a proud, sensual Tuscan peasant woman holding her stomach. We are intruders interrupting her reverie as she considers the enormous and tragic implications of her pregnancy. There are no distractions. The figures are statuesque and impassive, the colours restricted to blues, greens and purple-pinks. The perfect stillness of the scene, enhanced by the symmetrical placing of the two angels, imbues the image with a universal quality. The painting's strongest appeal is not, however, to art historians, but, appropriately enough, to the pregnant women of Monterchi, who continue to come here, as they have done ever since it was painted, to ask for the Madonna's intercession during childbirth.

Piero's monumental fresco of the Risen Christ hangs in the Town Hall of Borgo Sansepolcro. It is an austere work of great power.

The monumental feeling Piero captures is equally evident in the fresco of the Resurrection that Piero painted for the Palazzo Comunale in the sleepy town of Borgo Sansepolcro. From Monterchi head back towards Arezzo and turn right on the SS73 to Sansepolcro. It is a little disconcerting to find such an austere religious work painted on the wall of the inconspicuous town hall, now the Pinacoteca, and not in a church. However, the subject may refer to the Resurrected Christ who appears on the coat of arms of Sansepolcro, a town which claimed a mythical affinity with the site of the Holy Sepulchre. Its secular setting in no way lessens the impact of the painting.

In the cold light of dawn, while four soldiers are deep in slumber, the severe figure of Christ rises silently from his tomb. The motionless figure, with his stern, unbending gaze, transfixes the spectator. The power that emanates from him is similar to that of the finest Byzantine mosaics, and it is just possible that Piero may have visited Ravenna while working in nearby Rimini. To symbolize the Redeemer's re-birth, the trees in the landscape are divided into two groups, the dead ones are to the left while those on the right sprout greenery. The sleeping soldier in a classical breastplate, leaning his head against the rim of the tomb, is traditionally said to be a self-portrait.

Two damaged fragments of St Julian and St Louis of Toulouse and Piero's early polyptych of the Madonna della Misericordia also hang in the Pinacoteca. The polyptych, no longer in its original frame, is an uneven work, painted at various times between 1445 and 1460, much of it by the artist's pupils. However, the statuesque central figure of the Madonna as Mother of Mercy, standing out against the gold backdrop and enfolding the inhabitants of Sansepolcro who kneel beneath her all-enveloping cloak, possesses the hieratic quality of so much of his best work.

The apse of the church of San Francesco in Arezzo contains Piero's fresco cycle of the Legend of the True Cross. This is the best place to admire his colours and his mastery of composition.

The final cycle of paintings by Piero on this itinerary lies in the church of San Francesco in the busy mercantile town of Arezzo. (Once again, at the time of writing, half of them are celebrating Piero's quincentenary by standing invisible behind scaffolding.) To reach Arezzo, head west from Sansepolcro on the SS73 for 36km.

In a world of constantly changing values, the one immutable element is the timing of an Italian sacristan's lunch, and you can be sure that the church of San Francesco will shut at 12 o'clock on the dot. After a decent siesta he should be willing to let you in at about three in the afternoon. You may therefore prefer to make a leisurely exploration of Arezzo, lunching in the Buca di San Francesco next to the church, or in one of the many restaurants in the handsome Piazza Grande, and wait for the church to reopen.

In either event, the grandiose cycle filling the choir should not be hurried. The figures are painted on a large scale and placed at the front of the picture plane so as to be easily distinguishable, unlike so many medieval frescoes. This is just as well, because Piero, or more likely the Franciscans who commissioned the paintings, chose an immensely complex subject. The cycle depicts the Legend of the True Cross, a rather obscure and fanciful subject for a Renaissance artist, deeply imbued with the spirit of humanism.

The narrative opens with the Death of Adam; the tree that grew on his tomb (top of right wall), and was later recognized by the Queen of Sheba (centre of right wall), was subsequently used for Christ's Crucifixion (not represented). Centuries later, the Cross appeared in a dream to Constantine (right side of altar wall) on the night before his victory over Maxentius (bottom of right wall). Constantine's mother Helena then dug up the Cross (centre of left wall); the Persian King Chosroes looted it, but it was recovered in battle by the Emperor Heraclius (bottom of left wall), who restored it to Jerusalem (top of left wall).

With such disparate material, Piero succeeded in creating a series of paintings which rival Masaccio's work in the Brancacci Chapel in Florence as the

Right: The 'Madonna del Parto' by Piero della Francesca hangs in a little wayside chapel outside the village of Monterchi.

Opposite: Pedestrians hurry past the Romanesque Pieve di Santa Maria adjoining the Piazza Grande in Arezzo.

supreme fresco cycle of the Quattrocento. The right wall is the more impressive, particularly the central scene of 'The Queen of Sheba adoring the Holy Wood and the Meeting of Solomon and the Queen of Sheba'. Piero displays his mastery of composition on a grand scale; his figures, clothed in his favourite rose-reds, greens and silvery-whites, their gestures grave and respectful, give the events a suitable solemnity. To the left a pair of grooms, holding their mistress's horses in the landscape, provide a touch of humanity to offset the ceremonial severity of the central group.

The 'Victory of Constantine over Maxentius' below, although damaged, depicts the Emperor and his troops marching to battle through the ravishing landscape of the Tuscan-Umbrian border with a silvery river winding into the distance. In the 'Dream of Constantine', on the altar wall, a highly original night scene, recognized by Vasari for its 'skill and art', Piero creates a dream-like atmosphere through the subtle lighting emanating from the flying angel, and centred on the sleeping figure of the emperor in his tent. In both frescoes the figure of Constantine is probably a portrait of the Greek Emperor John Palaeologus, whom Piero would doubtless have seen at the Council of Florence in 1439. The lower scenes on both sides of the apse depict battle scenes between Christians and infidels, a potent theme at the time, since Constantinople, the eastern capital of Christendom for a thousand years, fell to the Turks in 1453, a year after Piero probably began work on the fresco cycle.

Experts are divided on the chronology of the cycle, but it was almost certainly painted between 1452 and 1466, and mostly between 1454 and 1458, when Piero was at the height of his powers. All the lessons that he had learnt in Florence have been assimilated. However structurally conceived – and art historians have wasted much ink poring over the intellectual abstractions of the placement of each figure, tree and building under the influence of Alberti's theories – the compositions are easily understandable to the layman. The statuesque figures, demonstrating Piero's knowledge of human anatomy, stand naturally in their settings and are defined by the space surrounding them. They are painted in a muted range of colours. Their draperies are very simple and the architecture behind them virtually unadorned. Although the cycle does contain portraits of contemporary figures, the majority are idealized and their beauty is far removed from the everyday world.

The rest of the frescoes in San Francesco pale in comparison with the Piero cycle. However, if you turn left out of the church and follow Via Cavour down to the Badia, the next church on the left, the fresco of St Lawrence by Bartolomeo della Gatta, just inside the main door, is a powerful figure holding his grill, almost as imposing as the figures of Piero himself. Returning to San Francesco, head north up Via Cesalpino to the Duomo. In the dark Gothic interior, far up the left aisle next to the sacristy door, Piero frescoed the monumental figure of the Magdalen, the only one of his later works in Arezzo to survive. She is as solid as a piece of sculpture, dominating the niche in which she stands. The light that falls from the left models the Magdalen's green dress and red cloak, and the jar of ointment in her left hand.

Neglected on the Grand Tour, and virtually unknown until this century, Piero stands at the climax of Quattrocento painting. The high-minded gravity of his figures, so unlike the decorative exuberance of his Florentine contemporaries, seems closer to our modern approach to art. Although one can recognize in Piero's figures the country people of his own day, and the landscape is clearly that of the Tuscan-Umbrian border, his paintings are universal and timeless. His home province remains a haven of peace, and you can still wander through the landscapes of the upper Tiber valley and see the ruddy peasant women working in the fields, just as Piero must have seen them as he rode his horse through the low wooded hills from Sansepolcro down to Monterchi and on to Arezzo.

TOUR 2

THE GARDEN AS THEATRE

VILLA REALE, MARLIA · VILLA MANSI, SEGROMIGNO · VILLA TORRIGIANI, CAMIGLIANO
VILLA GARZONI, COLLODI

The Villa Reale at Marlia possesses the finest garden near Lucca. The green theatre, hidden behind a high yew hedge, is one of the triumphs of baroque gardening.

Starting-point: Villa Reale, Marlia

Recommended time: A day and a half

Length of tour: 12 miles (20km)

Best time of year: May

Finishing-point: Villa Garzoni, Collodi

One of the best kept secrets in Italy is the splendour of its formal gardens, so many of which survive in their original state. The baroque gardeners of the seventeenth century were inspired to emulate the extraordinary achievements of their Renaissance predecessors (see page 43), and created a series of masterpieces all over the peninsula.

Four of these gardens lie in the green hills north of the charming walled town of Lucca. Blessed with a fertile soil, and an ample rainfall (visitors be warned: green countryside as depicted in posters and postcards invariably means lots of rain), and with the backdrop of a dramatic range of mountains, the Lucchesia is ideally suited to the construction of gardens. The Lucchese nobility, with the profits from their banking and mercantile activities, and from their large land holdings, created a series of splendid gardens during a prolonged period of peace and prosperity, from the sixteenth century to the eighteenth, coinciding with the age of the baroque.

In these gardens, the imagination is given a much freer rein than in the ideal, formalized world of the Renaissance. The gardeners enjoyed playing with the classical orders, introducing broken balustrades, oval shapes and animated sculpture to provide a sense of movement. Spaces merge, symmetry is no longer all-important, and there is no rigorous boundary separating the garden from the surrounding countryside. Baroque gardeners loved artificial effects, tricks that would delight or horrify the unsuspecting visitor. Surprise vistas open up around every corner, water jokes abound, and a maze is often introduced, to further dumbfound the guests.

If you are pushed for time, or a slow starter, try not to miss the Villa Reale at Marlia, some 8km north of Lucca, just to the right of the road to Barga, which follows the right bank of the River Serchio. It can be visited in a morning, leaving the afternoon for the Villa Torrigiani and the Villa Mansi. Alternatively, the afternoon can be spent in the Villa Garzoni, an extravagant display of ostentation which gives the best overall idea of the baroque garden. Unfortunately, the seventeenth-century layout of the first three was radically altered by the nineteenth-century Italian passion for the English-style garden. However, in every case, a large section of the original plan survives.

The grounds of the Villa Reale are very large, combining an informal garden with a baroque set piece and a delightful green theatre. The lawn that stretches out in front of the villa was laid out in 1811-14 by Morel, the architect of the villa, for Elisa Baciocchi, the libertine sister of Napoleon, who purchased the villa from the Orsini family. It has been subtly landscaped with sunken paths to allow a vista of uninterrupted greenery down to the ornamental lake. Morel planted the trees and shrubs flanking the lawn to provide constant variety.

At the bottom of the garden by the lake is the old palace of the bishops of Lucca, now sadly dilapidated. Beyond it stands the Grotto of Pan, built in 1570-80, paved in different coloured stones and pebble mosaics, and filled with sculpture of tritons and dolphins, and the usual repertoire of hearty water jokes, an essential component of Italian formal gardens. After a while you can become expert at working out where the levers tend to be hidden in grottoes and test out your fellow tourists' sense of humour (often surprisingly poor) for yourself. Behind the grotto a Spanish-style garden, laid out in the 1920s in a

Opposite: The full baroque magnificence of the Villa Garzoni at Collodi – a feast of garden statuary, ramped staircases and a water cascade. Top: A river god reclines nonchalantly beside a *nymphaeum* at the Villa Reale, Marlia. Below: Gesticulating statues on the façade of the Villa Mansi are dramatically silhouetted against gathering storm clouds.

The Villa Mansi at Segromigno has some handsome trees in an English-style informal garden. Beyond lie the remains of Juvarra's water garden.

deliberate evocation of the Generalife in Granada, is in a rather mournful state of decay.

Beyond, hidden behind a high ilex hedge, lies the most magical baroque garden in the whole of Italy, culminating in an exquisite green theatre. It lies at the end of a series of three outdoor rooms, all set on axis, with heavily rusticated gate piers. The first of these, filled with lemon trees, is designed on a cross-axis, with a *nymphaeum* at each end, and a rectangular pool, on which white swans glide. The *nymphaea*, attributed to the great Turinese architect Juvarra, show a baroque delight in different textures, the rough white stone contrasting with the clean lines of the sculpture and the still water of the pool. The statues are personifications of the Rivers Arno and Serchio, and, appropriately, a group of Leda and the Swan. The second room is circular, with a tall fountain silhouetted against the dark yews. The plume of water serves as a useful means of concealing the theatre.

The third room, planted in 1652, is the *pièce de résistance*. High yew hedges enclose the spectator, whose gaze is focused on the stage, peopled by terracotta figures from the *commedia dell' arte*. On either side, the hedges have been cut to allow the players to enter and exit unseen. Box topiary conceals the lights at the front of the stage, and the prompter standing beneath. Windows have been cut in the hedges facing the stage to increase the illusion that we are at the theatre. The overall effect is intimate and entrancing, and one can easily imagine Pulchinello and Colombina appearing on stage, or Paganini playing to Elisa and her paramour Bartolomeo Cenami, reclining on their chaise-longues.

As so often in Italian garden design, the architect made use of a slight rise in the lie of the land to place the stage above the spectators. This ability to mould a garden to the landscape was very often ignored by the imitators of the Italian format, so that many a European monarch bankrupted himself in trying to emulate the fountains in the great Renaissance gardens on flat ground, where there is no natural pressure to push the water upwards. Nothing else at Marlia rivals this masterpiece of garden design, surprisingly by an unknown architect. The villa itself is no more than a plain neoclassical box, and the water garden behind is one of any number of rockeries in Italy.

From Marlia, a back road runs due east for 5km to the Villa Mansi at Segromigno. The original architect, Muzio Oddi, designed the building as a rectangular block in the 1630s, but Giovan Francesco Giusti's addition of balustrades and statues in the 1740s, and his raising of the central block of one storey, completely altered the character of the villa. Giusti gave the building the variety and movement so typical of the baroque, and submerged the main motif of Palladio's favourite Serlian window beneath any number of statues and broken pediments.

The Cenami family, who had commissioned Oddi, sold the villa to Ottavio Mansi in 1675, and it was he who asked Juvarra to lay out the garden between 1725 and 1732. Only the water garden near the stable block survives from his ambitious scheme, which was destroyed when the landscape was replanted in an informal English style in the nineteenth century.

Your attention is initially focused on the swathe of lawn in front of the villa, flanked by handsome specimen trees, including the best group of tulip trees I have ever seen. Wandering past these you come across the remnants of Juvarra's water garden. A cascade runs down to an octagonal basin, surrounded by a balustrade surmounted by statues. Openings are cut in the balustrade to focus the spectator's eye on the vista up the hillside. Adjoining the pond is the remains of a sunken garden with another, murky pond. Legend has it that this was where the sinister Lucinda Mansi, who, like Dorian Gray, sold her soul to the devil to preserve her beauty, used to come to bathe.

The Villa Torrigiani at Camigliano is approached up a long cypress avenue. It has an interesting, sunken water garden.

Almost next door to the Villa Mansi lies the Villa Torrigiani at Camigliano. The approach is very dramatic, with the villa silhouetted between heavily rusticated gate piers at the top of a long avenue of cypresses, many of which are, sadly, diseased. The façade, attributed to Oddi, is even more intricate than that of the Villa Mansi. Gesticulating statues of every shape and size embellish the multi-coloured front, with its rough stonework and smooth plaster, making it look like some indigestible wedding cake. The interior is something of a hotch-potch, apart from some interesting mythological paintings by Batoni. These are particularly fascinating for the British, since Batoni, who came from Lucca, went on to become the most sought-after portraitist of Grand Tourists.

The lawn, trees and shrubs in front of the villa were laid out in the nineteenth century, with the exception of two irregular pools, but the French-style sunken garden to the right survives from the seventeenth century, when the owner, Marquis Niccolò Santini, was Lucca's ambassador to the court of Louis XIV. A terrace, with a fishpond and lemon trees on one side, overlooks a sunken garden of Flora, hidden from the villa. A mass of jets of water lie concealed at the end of the parterre. Retreating in disarray, the unfortunate visitor seeks refuge in the grotto, where a barrage of water jets spurts from the floor, ceiling and walls.

The Villa Garzoni has a wonderful, full-blown formal baroque garden with terraces, fountains, statues and a maze.

Overleaf: Dawn mist enshrouds isolated farmhouses in the bare Tuscan landscape near Monte Oliveto.

The final garden is at Collodi, some 17km east of Lucca on the SS435. The Villa Garzoni is laid out on a steep hillside, a perfect backdrop for the baroque love of scene setting. The main terraces were laid out in the seventeenth century, and embellished by Ottaviano Diodati in 1786. The operatic staircases and the central water cascade look back to Bramante and Vignola, but they are intentionally more grandiose, and more closely integrated with the surrounding woods. The gigantic, overblown statue of Fame, spurting a jet of water through her trumpet from the top of the cascade towards the figures of

Florence and Lucca, seems to emerge from the ilex trees. The terracotta statues of peasants and monkeys, interspersed with mythological figures, emphasize the garden's integration with the natural world.

Baroque gardens were designed to hold crowds, and therefore laid out on a grander scale than their Renaissance counterparts. The large, lower terrace is devoted to the favourite baroque theme of showing off the pomp and grandeur of the ruling family. Some of the beds are adorned with the Garzoni coat of arms laid out in brightly coloured gravel, and two circular pools with fountains shooting high into the air, which show a mastery of water effects. All sorts of devices create the effect of movement. The diagonal staircase, the cascade leading to Fame, the fountains, the intricate patterns of the box hedges – all keep the eye in constant motion. Even the yew hedges by the entrance are clipped in curves and scrolls. Ignoring the bright red salvias and other annuals so offensive to those brought up to pay homage to the pastel shades of Gertrude Jekyll and Vita Sackville-West, one can see why this was regarded as the outstanding garden in Tuscany, a vital stop for Grand Tourists such as William Beckford. So impressed was Charles III of Naples that he wanted to employ Diodati to lay out the gardens at Caserta.

On the left of the water cascade a path runs through the *bosco* over a stream. From here you can descend to admire the baroque integration of art and nature as the maze (fiendishly difficult for those who enjoy getting lost) emerges from the clumps of bamboo which, in turn, lead to the green theatre. The path above continues past statues of Samson and Hercules up to the villa. Its curious castellated exterior, with its baroque convex and concave curves, constructed in the early seventeenth century, gives little indication of the charming summerhouse behind, or the fine frescoes by Mengozzi Colonna, *trompe-l'oeil* expert and collaborator of Tiepolo (see page 74). It was in this villa in the nineteenth century that Carlo Lorenzini conceived the immensely popular if gruesome character of Pinocchio.

BEACONS OF CIVILIZATION

SANT' ANTIMO · MONTE OLIVETO · SAN GALGANO

The beautiful abbey of Sant' Antimo stands in a wonderful position. It has retained a very strong atmosphere. Decoration, both inside and outside, has been kept to a minimum.

Starting-point: Sant' Antimo

Recommended time:

Full day

Length of tour: 62 miles

(100km)

Best time of year: April/June

or September/October

Finishing-point: San Galgano

During the Middle Ages, the light of civilization was kept burning by the religious orders. Although many of them withdrew from the world into tight, self-contained communities, they exerted a major influence through their teaching and learning. Their knowledge of classical literature, their understanding of medicine, and their skill in the arts of illumination and calligraphy, kept these ancient arts and sciences alive.

The monastic ideal, so difficult for us to comprehend, was enormously important. In a society where God was all-powerful, the monastic life was seen as a sure route to salvation. The orders attracted vast donations, both from cynics who wished to safeguard their own souls and from those who genuinely responded to the inspirational preaching of St Francis and St Dominic. With this wealth the orders were able to erect a series of magnificent abbeys and monasteries throughout central Italy. Three of the most splendid of these are situated in southern Tuscany.

Like so many of these foundations, the Benedictine abbey of Sant' Antimo stands in an isolated position some 8km south of the hill-town of Montalcino. It is difficult to imagine a more beautiful position than this, hidden in a bowl in the Tuscan hills. The abbey is pure French Romanesque, and reflects the wide-ranging influence of Cluny in Burgundy, which, under the impetus of a series of remarkable abbots, became the spiritual capital of Europe. The verticality of the nave, the clerestory, and the ambulatory running behind the altar with its curious alabaster columns and windows, and radiating chapels, all derive from France.

The abbey is supposed to have been founded by Charlemagne in 781, in fulfilment of a vow he had made to stop the plague which decimated his army as it passed Monte Amiata. The present construction was begun in 1118, and completed during the twelfth century, when Sant' Antimo became one of the most powerful abbeys in Tuscany. It was suppressed by Pius II in 1462. After years of neglect, during which almost all the monastic buildings disappeared, some Augustinian monks have taken over the buildings. The best time to visit is on a Sunday afternoon when they sing their Gregorian chant. My only criticism of the abbey concerns the replacement of many of the capitals in the nave; you can spot the new ones quite clearly if you compare their quality, and state of preservation, with the wonderfully vibrant carving of Daniel in the Lion's Den on the second capital on the right.

From Sant' Antimo, head back to Montalcino, passing fields covered in the vines which produce Brunello wine, a much superior and more intoxicating wine than Chianti, with which it is often confused. Just before Montalcino, you pass the Biondi Santi vineyard, which produces the most famous (and expensive) Brunello wine. This is probably the only Italian red which stands comparison with the best vintages from Piedmont. Vines have been grown here since the Middle Ages. Medieval monks loved their drink, concocting Dom Perignon champagne and Benedictine long before their secular brethren had put away their cups of mead.

Beyond Montalcino, from where Leonardo is reputed to have drawn his bird's-eye view of the world, the road snakes downhill until you turn left on to the Via Cassia. This was once one of the main roads in the Roman Empire, linking the Imperial capital with the provinces north of the Alps. During the Middle Ages, Siena gained much of her wealth from her position on this road between Rome and Florence. Now it is scarcely used, and the magnificent, arid landscape is almost deserted apart from the occasional shepherd and farmstead. With the collapse of the *mezzadria* system (under which the landowner and tenant divided the produce of the soil), after the last war, the land is undercultivated. As the smaller fields have disappeared, so the scale of the vistas across the chalky soil, known as the *cratere senese*, have assumed the vastness of the landscape of Africa.

The isolated monastery of Monte Oliveto emerges from a grove of cypresses. The great cloister has an important cycle of frescoes by Signorelli and Sodoma depicting the life of St Benedict.

At Buonconvento, turn right for Monte Oliveto. The impressive complex of monastic buildings rises from amid some superb cypresses. In this secluded setting Bernardo Tolomei, the scion of one of Siena's most noble families, founded his Olivetan Order, a branch of the Benedictines, in 1319, six years after he had turned his back on his aristocratic roots. He advocated a more austere and literal observance of the Benedictine Rule, a sparse diet without meat, continuous silence and regular manual work. The Olivetans were one of the last of a series of reforming orders which appeared throughout the Middle Ages, dedicated to following a life of hardship and poverty in an attempt to combat the growing religious dissent and anti-clericalism in the towns, and to recapture the simple lifestyle of the Apostles. Needless to say, they tended to attract recruits from the affluent classes and the clerical intelligentsia rather than peasants and serfs, who were astounded that anyone could be foolish enough to choose a life of unremitting toil.

The ruined Cistercian abbey of San Galgano is situated in lonely countryside south-west of Siena, one of the most romantic sites in Tuscany.

However, the Olivetan Order enjoyed immediate success and, in order to capitalize on its fame, a series of frescoes of the life of St Benedict were commissioned for the walls of the great cloister at the end of the fifteenth century. They were begun by Signorelli in 1497-8 and completed by Sodoma in 1505-8. The frescoes show the impact of antiquity, even in this remote outpost, in the classical architecture that appears in the background of the scenes, and in the grotesque decoration of the panels in between the episodes, reflecting the influence of the recent dis-

covery of Nero's Golden House in Rome. The artists indulged their sense of humour to the full, delighting in the depiction of the devils who torment the monks by tempting them with seductive women, knock down the buildings that they erect, and constantly attempt to sabotage St Benedict's miracles. In keeping with the beauty of the surrounding countryside, Sodoma shows his skill in the feathery landscapes that fill his backgrounds.

The architecture of the monastery is not particularly remarkable, apart from the fine double staircase leading up to the library, but the church contains some of the finest *intarsia* work in central Italy. The craftsmanship of Giovanni da Verona is exquisite, showing a sophistication in the treatment of the different woods that is quite astonishing. For instance the black wood comes from 'drowned oak', produced by leaving the wood under water for several years until it is exactly the right colour. The actual scenes show off the artist's knowledge of perspective and *trompe-l'oeil*, as he effortlessly conjures up images of still lives, musical instruments, globes, birds and model towns. Occasionally, these are recognizable, as in a view of Siena with the Palazzo Pubblico. In the centre of the church a three-tiered lectern is decorated with *trompe-l'oeil* illuminated manuscripts, and a most realistic cat.

The third of the splendid abbeys in southern Tuscany lies in a lonely spot of great beauty. Return to Buonconvento, head back to Siena, and take the SS73 towards Grosseto. The approach from Siena begins by passing through an open landscape of fields of rich red earth (which gives its name to burnt sienna), planted with maize and vines, before entering a thickly wooded valley of ilex, arbutus and broom. Beyond Frosini a winding road descends into a plain; San Galgano lies off the SS439 immediately after the road branches off towards Follonico.

The abbey is the major Cistercian foundation in Tuscany, and was built between 1212 and 1288. Once again, as at Sant' Antimo, the French influence is

Above: The simple beauty of the Benedictine abbey of Sant' Antimo, surrounded by olive trees. Opposite: The monastery of Monte Oliveto, set among a grove of cypresses, rises above the early morning mist.

ruptibility stood it in good stead. The Cistercians played a major role in Sienese history, fostering the republic's links with France, and providing the Chamberlain or Treasurer for the city's important Biccherna, or department of finance. The Gothic style of San Galgano proved highly influential in giving Siena its distinctive Gothic appearance, and from 1258 to 1285 the Master of Works of the Duomo was a monk from San Galgano, who commissioned Nicola Pisano's pulpit, one of the city's greatest artistic treasures.

The abbey fell into decay during the Renaissance, and the roof collapsed following the dissolution of the monastery in 1652. But its ruined appearance, with grass growing in the nave, merely enhances its romantic appeal. Some monks still remain, and the sight of them in their white habits going about their duties summons up visions of their forebears teaching in the cloister, sitting in silence in the refectory during meals while one of the brethren read from the pulpit, meeting in the chapter house, and trooping in to the great abbey to celebrate Lauds, Prime, Terce and Vespers. In such a peaceful setting, under a strict discipline, they were able to concentrate on worshipping God and preserving the essence of their civilization.

The abbey itself is built in a picturesque mixture of travertine and red brick. A simple altar on miniature columns stands at the centre of the crossing. Many of the details, particularly the façade and the capitals in the nave, are very weathered, but, considering the centuries of neglect, its survival is almost miraculous. A small circular Romanesque church, dating from 1182-5, which can easily be reached by walking up the hill, contains fragments of frescoes by Ambrogio Lorenzetti. In the middle stands a stone into which San Galgano plunged his sword in repudiation of his military prowess. Considering the romance surrounding the whole site, this is an almost surreal Arthurian touch, and one half expects to see the once and future king appearing at the door of the church.

paramount, only here it is the soaring arches of the Gothic rather than the Romanesque. The Cistercians represent the next reforming wave of monasticism, following on from the Benedictines of Cluny. As a sign of their austerity they adopted a coarse habit of undyed sheep's wool, and set up secluded foundations on deserted and uncultivated land, far from inhabited settlements. San Galgano is a typical example of this, standing alone, surrounded by fields of sunflowers, with only an occasional farm worker on his tractor to disturb the calm and remind one of the twentieth century.

The order's reputation for austerity and incor-

TOUR 4

MEDICI MAGNIFICENCE

PRATO · POGGIO A CAIANO · CARMIGNANO · ARTIMINO

The Romanesque Duomo at Prato possesses an excellent fresco cycle by Filippo Lippi and a frieze sculpted for the pulpit by Donatello.

The Medici name is indelibly linked with the city of Florence. Controlling Florentine culture as well as politics, Cosimo de' Medici and his grandson Lorenzo Il Magnifico patronized and befriended the greatest scholars, artists and writers of the day. With their encouragement, Florentine artists dominated Italian art, producing an ideal of beauty which captivated all Europe. Many of their finest works still remain in the city, but a surprising number are situated in towns and villages in the surrounding countryside.

In a day's excursion west of Florence, and with the inestimable advantage of avoiding the hordes congregated in the city's museums and churches, you can discover some of the outstanding works of the Renaissance in the town of Prato, and in the hills ranging to the south, where these humanist princes were equally at home out hunting or engaging in philosophical discussions.

Prato, despite its proximity to Florence, has flourished on the proceeds of the cloth trade for centuries. Once you have passed the eyesore of its suburbs, the centre is still a pretty market town of yellow and cream façades with green shutters, where you are more likely to be held up by a small boy on a bicycle setting off fishing than you are by a busload of tourists. The town possesses two masterpieces from the time of Cosimo Il Vecchio, both designed for the Romanesque Duomo, with its characteristically Tuscan green and white stripes: a fresco cycle by Filippo Lippi, and a frieze designed by Donatello for the pulpit on the façade.

Both these artists were favourites of Cosimo. Donatello he treated like his own son, dressing him in fine clothes, much to the artist's disgust, and giving him a farm near his villa at Caffagiolo. (Donatello is

one of many Italian artists with nicknames – his means little Donato.) Fra Filippo Lippi was an extraordinary contradiction, a monk who lived life to the full, forever drinking and pursuing pretty women; at one point he fled from his vows only to fall into the arms of some Barbary pirates. His ardent pursuit of the fair sex led Cosimo to order him to be locked into his bedroom at night. But Lippi had tied his sheets together and was shinning down the wall before the key had turned in the lock. Just as the popes of his era made their sons cardinals, so Lippi fathered a son, Filippino, who was to become one of the leading Florentine painters of the fifteenth century.

Lippi's masterly frescoes of the Lives of St John the Baptist and St Stephen, dating from 1452 to 1466, fill the walls behind the high altar in the choir of the Duomo. On the left wall are scenes from the life of St Stephen, which are rather obscure, except for one, in the corner, which is instantly recognizable as the Stoning. On the right wall we are on firmer ground, with the Birth of St John at the top, his Wanderings in the Desert in the middle, and his Martyrdom at the bottom.

The frescoes include a number of excellent portraits, and some superb rocky landscapes in the backgrounds to the depictions of St Stephen receiving Bishop Julian's blessing, and of St John preaching in the desert. The portraits include Carlo de' Medici, the illegitimate son of Cosimo by a Circassian slave, who appears in the Funeral of St Stephen. Bastardy held no stigma at a Renaissance court (indeed Lorenzo Il Magnifico's illegitimate nephew became Pope Clement VII), and Carlo was elected Provost of Prato cathedral. The most famous fresco in the cycle is the Martyrdom of the Baptist, in which Herod sits

Starting-point: Prato
Recommended time:
Full day
Length of tour: 15 miles
(24km)
Best time of year: May or
October
Finishing-point: Artimino

transfixed by the swirling figure of the dancing Salome, one of the most delightful images in Quattrocento painting.

These frescoes were instantly recognized for their genius. The city of Prato, well pleased that it had managed to entice such a renowned Florentine artist away from his home town, gave Lippi 2,400 florins. And, as a measure of his appreciation, Cosimo managed to obtain a dispensation from the pope for Filippo to marry his mistress Lucrezia Buti, a beautiful young novice.

Nothing else in the Duomo matches these frescoes. Those attributed to Uccello in the neighbouring chapel pale in comparison, as do those by Agnolo Gaddi in the chapel by the main door. Even Mino da Fiesole's pretty reliefs around the pulpit and Giovanni Pisano's Madonna and Child over the high altar cannot compete. The only work that rivals Lippi's in excellence is Donatello's frieze of Dancing Putti, dating from 1428-38, which originally decorated Michelozzo's pulpit. From this pulpit the Holy Girdle of the Virgin, dropped at Doubting Thomas's feet on her Assumption, was exhibited on certain feast days to the multitude gathered in the piazza. The sculpture has now been replaced by a copy and stands in the museum next door.

Donatello's frieze, like his better-known Cantoria (singing gallery) in the Museo dell' Opere del Duomo in Florence, is a Bacchanalian riot of movement. A group of high-spirited children race round in a circle, blowing trumpets, pulling each other's hair, and dashing in every direction. They are carved in relief, but done so subtly that Donatello achieves a real sense of depth.

Prato is worth wandering through, but if you want to explore the two Medici villas to the south, and Pontormo's 'Visitation' at Carmignano, you will be able to spare no more than a quick glance at Giuliano da Sangallo's centrally planned Santa Maria delle Carceri, dating from 1485, and named after a miraculous image of the Madonna which appeared on a prison wall (*carcere* in Italian). The church

suffers from a constricted site, hemmed in by buildings and surrounded by traffic, but the elegant interior, with its harmonious proportions and its Andrea della Robbia enamel terracottas, derives from Brunelleschi, the greatest architect of the early Quattrocento. Giuliano's use of the Greek cross plan was taken up by several architects of the next generation, including Bramante, and his cousin Antonio da Sangallo the Elder whose masterpiece stands beneath the church of San Biagio at Montepulciano (see page 40).

Giuliano da Sangallo was the favourite architect of Lorenzo de' Medici, and in 1480 he was chosen to rebuild the Villa of Poggio a Caiano, south of Prato. This was a highly prestigious commission. Not only were the Medici the ruling family of Florence, but Lorenzo was following his grandfather Cosimo in setting a new fashion by building a villa where he could relax from the strains of life in the city and enjoy the benefits of nature. He loved riding, hawking, breeding his favourite racehorses, pigs and pheasants, and planting mulberry trees. Much of Lorenzo's most delightful bucolic poetry, showing his response to the beauty of nature, was inspired by the countryside around Poggio a Caiano. This was also where Lorenzo's Platonic Academy, under the leadership of Lorenzo himself, and his friends Poliziano and Pico della Mirandola, used to meet. It is difficult for us to conceive that, before this era, it was almost unknown for anyone to want to live in the countryside, unless it was in a fortified castle.

Sangallo designed Poggio a Caiano as a simple block, so typical of Tuscan villas, but inserted a classical temple front into the main façade, probably the first time that this was done in the Renaissance. Although the effect is rather cramped, this feature reflects the growing interest in antiquity, and was to be immensely influential on later architects, particularly Palladio. This interest in antiquity is equally evident in the terracotta frieze by Andrea Sansovino and

Poggio a Caiano was Lorenzo Il Magnifico's favourite villa. Pontormo painted his delightful fresco of Vertumnus and Pomona in the grand *salone*.

Giuliano da Sangallo, originally on the temple front, and now standing inside, which is inspired by classical prototypes, both in its form and in its neo-Platonic theme.

The interior of the villa is almost bare. There are some interesting rooms on the ground floor decorated in the nineteenth century, including a little theatre and a billiard room with a fresco of a pergola with cupids playing. Upstairs, the grand *salone* was frescoed by Andrea del Sarto, Pontormo, Franciabigio and Alessandro Allori, all favoured artists of the Medici. The room is dedicated to the glory of the Medici, with scenes from ancient Rome reflecting episodes from their own history.

Pontormo's famous fresco of Vertumnus and Pomona, painted in 1521, and commissioned by the pleasure-loving Medici Pope Leo X, the son of Lorenzo, is a pastoral idyll, with elegant ladies, labourers enjoying a picnic and youths picking grapes, all at ease with nature. Inspired by the Pope, and by the efforts of the other artists participating in the cycle, Pontormo's fresco is one of his freshest works, very unlike his highly disturbing altar-pieces. Following the Pope's death in 1521, the expulsion of the Medici and the destructive Siege of Florence in 1529-30, Pontormo never completed the decorative scheme of the villa.

Poggio a Caiano has remained substantially unchanged since the time of Leo and Pontormo, although the horseshoe-shaped staircase curving up to the front door is a baroque addition. The villa was popular with the Medici Grand Dukes. Bianca Cappello, the beautiful mistress of Francesco I, died of malaria here shortly after the Grand Duke had expired, although legend has it that they were both poisoned. Later the high-spirited Marguerite-Louise d'Orléans fled here from her husband Cosimo III, outraging society by tickling the French cook and galloping through the woods. The garden was transformed into the informal, English style in the nineteenth century, largely by King Victor Emmanuel II and his wife. Like so many of the Medici villas, it is no longer set in true countryside, but it has retained more of its setting than Poggio Imperiale, Pratolino, Castello and Careggi, all of which have been impaired by their proximity to the suburbs of Florence.

The church of San Michele at Carmignano contains Pontormo's 'Visitation', a disturbing work by this strange and original Mannerist painter.

To appreciate the proper relationship of a villa with its surroundings, you need to venture south from Poggio a Caiano to Artimino, taking in en route the Pontormo altar-piece in Carmignano, which lies 5km to the west. The church of San Michele appears an unassuming building with little to recommend it apart from a charming fifteenth-century cloister, whose *pietra serena* columns contrast with the rustic feel of the olives growing among them. This unprepossessing air is enhanced by the small boys on bicycles racing round the cloister, past the Fiat parked in one corner, and the workman restoring furniture in the baroque chapel which leads off it.

This unlikely backdrop adds to the element of surprise when you are confronted by Pontormo's 'Visitation' over the second altar on the right in the church. The picture was commissioned by the Pinadori family for their villa at Carmignano, and moved to the church in about 1740, where it has remained ever since. It was painted in 1528-30, when Pontormo was at the height of his powers, and is one of the truly great Mannerist paintings.

The Villa of Artimino stands in a beautiful rustic setting overlooking olive groves. It was built by Buontalenti for the Medici Grand Duke Ferdinand I as a hunting lodge.

Pontormo was a strange, original artist, an eccentric loner obsessed with his own ideas. This painting, executed immediately after the Sack of Rome in 1527, is a far cry from his Arcadian fresco in Poggio a Caiano. The 'Visitation' is a complex work, based on the relationship between four women. In the centre of the picture the Madonna and St Elizabeth, both pregnant, embrace, while behind them two women gaze fixedly out at the spectator. This contrast between the two pairs of figures, each seemingly un-

aware of the other, introduces a note of unease. The background is similarly disconcerting, the architecture difficult to understand, and two strange men appear on the right by a doorway. The brilliant blues, greens, pinks and yellows, painted with startling clarity, and the way that the figures are placed at the front of the picture plane, add to the impact of the painting. But the message is no longer one of harmony and beauty characteristic of the High Renaissance, and seems to bear out Vasari's description of Pontormo's 'bizarre and fantastic brain'.

From Carmignano, you continue to head southwest, deeper into the countryside. The road rises into the hills, flanked by cypresses, with vineyards lining the hillsides. Near Artimino these are replaced by thick oak woods interspersed with olive groves. The view spreads out over the Arno valley, which opens like a gigantic amphitheatre towards Florence and the other Medici villas. These were reproduced in Giusto Utens' delightful lunettes which once hung in the grand hall of Artimino (now in the Museo di Firenze Com'era).

The Villa of Artimino was built in the late sixteenth century by Buontalenti for the Grand Duke Ferdinand I, an able ruler who loved to relax from the cares of office by hunting game through the surrounding woods. The villa's low, graceful, rectangular block, punctuated by dozens of dovecotes, makes no pretensions to grandeur. No garden was constructed, because of the shortage of water, so that the villa emerges from the olive groves. As at Poggio a Caiano, a small portico has been inset into the façade, but it seems even more of an apology to the classical revival. The double curving staircase was added in this century, to a design by Buontalenti. If you have time, a short drive beyond the villa, through a dramatic landscape with a number of handsome umbrella pines, takes you down to the Arno. In this unspoilt countryside, it is easy to imagine both Lorenzo and Ferdinand joking and laughing with their friends as they set off for the chase.

TOUR 5

PILGRIMS' FOOTSTEPS

SANTA MARIA DELLA CONSOLAZIONE, TODI · MADONNA DI SAN BIAGIO, MONTEPULCIANO
SANTA MARIA DEL CALCINAIO, CORTONA

The centrally planned church of Santa Maria della Consolazione is one of the most harmonious buildings of the Renaissance. It stands just outside the hill-town of Todi.

The late fifteenth century marks a crucial turning-point in the history of Europe. In the minds of many, the Papacy had proved itself unworthy of its onerous duties. The traffic in indulgences, the widespread practices of simony and nepotism, where popes automatically created their nephews and children cardinals, and built palaces for their mistresses, caused a crisis of faith. The spread of education and the new-found confidence of the individual fostered anticlericalism and a profound disrespect for religious authority. People desired a simpler form of religion.

The Quattrocento marked the triumph of humanism and saw the birth of modern man, but the old fatalistic view of religion remained strong. This became more marked as the year 1500, seen by many as heralding the end of the world, approached. Natural disasters were regarded as just punishment for sins committed, the devil was a real presence, and most men believed themselves damned. Savonarola, in Florence, was one of many charismatic preachers to play on people's fears and desires, as Luther was to do so devastatingly in the succeeding generation. Traditionally, in Catholic ideology, the most approachable figure has been the Madonna, who has played the role of intercessor for sinners, the sick and the needy. In central Italy, a number of miracles and visions, reflecting people's primitive view of the supernatural, were reported and quickly became the focus of pilgrimages. To accommodate the faithful who flocked to these sites, churches were erected in the Virgin's honour.

Three of these pilgrimage churches lie within the vicinity of Lake Trasimene (and another stands in Prato – see page 34). Each of them stands just outside

a hill-town, filled with works of art, but I have concentrated on the churches and the spectacular views that they enjoy over the surrounding landscape. You can visit all three within a day providing you do not spend too much time in the adjoining towns. Alternatively, you can make two or three expeditions, taking in the numerous works of art in each individual town. The three churches make a fascinating contrast since their virgin sites encouraged the use of the central plan, a preoccupation of all leading architects throughout the Renaissance.

The most southerly of the three is the church of Santa Maria della Consolazione, just below the hilltop eyrie of Todi, with spectacular views in every direction across the rolling hills of south-west Umbria. The church, with its Greek cross plan, has been attributed to Bramante, but the light and graceful feel of the building has none of the monumentality of Bramante's Roman architecture. You could be forgiven for imagining that it dates from the Quattrocento, although it was not actually begun until 1508, and was finished a century later. The probable architect was the little-known Cola da Caprarola, and the church was completed after his death by the even more obscure Ambrogio Barocci and Francesco da Vita. They achieved a harmony of proportion and a sense of lightness typical of an earlier age, although certain features, such as the square balustrade jutting out beneath the dome, are a little awkward.

If you want to spend more time exploring Todi, the Piazza del Popolo, overlooked by the Duomo and a series of battlemented palaces, is very evocative of Umbria's medieval past. You can imagine the decrees of the Podesta being proclaimed from the steps of the Palazzo del Capitano, while city worthies crowded to

Starting-point: Santa Maria della Consolazione, Todi
Recommended time: Very full day or a day and a half
Length of tour: 76 miles (123km)
Best time of year: April/May or September/October
Finishing-point: Santa Maria del Calcinaio, Cortona

Right: Francesco di Giorgio's pilgrimage church of Santa Maria del Calcinaio stands among olive trees below the hill-town of Cortona.
Opposite: The magnificent interior of the Madonna di San Biagio, one of the greatest Renaissance buildings of central Italy.

The Madonna di San Biagio by Antonio da Sangallo ranks among the finest churches in central Italy. It is notable for its noble proportions and the beauty of its austere decoration.

listen from the windows of the neighbouring Palazzo del Popolo and the Palazzo dei Priori. Both the Duomo and San Fortunato, just beyond the piazza, have fine interiors, and the latter contains interesting fourteenth-century frescoes of the Life of St Francis and the Masolino of the Madonna and Child in chapels off the right aisle.

The second of the central Italian pilgrimage churches lies north-west of Todi in the Orcia valley. You can reach it by driving down the SS448 towards Orvieto, heading north up the *autostrada* to the Chiusi exit, and following the SS146 west past Chianciano Terme to Montepulciano. The pilgrimage church of the Madonna di San Biagio with its majestic dome, dating from 1518-45, stands in an isolated setting just below the town.

To my mind this ranks with the works of Brunelleschi as among the finest Renaissance churches in central Italy. Antonio da Sangallo the Elder, one of a large family of Florentine architects, made a close

study of the works of Brunelleschi and Bramante, and the drawings of Leonardo, all of whom had been fascinated by the classical symmetry of the centrally planned church. Sangallo's church combines the harmony of proportions typical of the Quattrocento with the monumentality of the High Renaissance. The brilliant white colour of the travertine stone, the austerity of the decoration, and the barrel vaults of the four arms of the Greek cross are all characteristic of Roman architecture and, in particular, the grandeur of the ancient Roman baths. It seems likely that this building captures most closely the initial design made by Bramante for St Peter's in 1506. The elegant Canonry beside the church, with its double loggia, is also by Sangallo.

Although Montepulciano is now a small, provincial town off the main route that runs from Florence to Rome, it played an important role in the Renaissance as the birthplace of Politian, the tutor of Lorenzo Il Magnifico and of Pope Marcellus II. As Cardinal Cervini del Vivo, Marcellus was a leading

figure in initiating the Counter-Reformation, and the patron of Palestrina, the papal composer. Montepulciano is filled with palaces dating from its era of greatness in the sixteenth century. Together with its neighbour Pienza, the creation of Pope Pius II, perched on the next hilltop to the west, it remains one of the most attractive hill-towns of central Italy.

Santa Maria del Calcinaio is another Renaissance pilgrimage church. Francesco di Giorgio's masterpiece stands just below Cortona. The interior possesses a wonderful feeling of space.

The third of the three pilgrimage churches stands on the edge of Cortona, an ancient Etruscan town overlooking the north shore of Lake Trasimene. This is a more formidable eyrie than Todi or Montepulciano, and from this vantage-point Hannibal and his Carthaginian troops plotted the downfall of the approaching Roman army at the battle of Lake Trasimene in 217BC.

The pilgrimage church of Santa Maria del Calcinaio lies at the foot of the town. It was built to commemorate the vision of the Madonna by a lime-burner in 1484. As at Todi and Montepulciano, pilgrims flocked to the site, and Francesco di Giorgio's masterpiece was erected between 1485 and 1513. From above, you can still capture the rural character of the church, set among the cypresses and olives, with the odd telephone wire intruding to spoil the perfect photograph.

The plain, weathered exterior, with its ribbed dome, gives little indication of the grandiose feeling of space inside. The Sienese architect and sculptor Francesco di Giorgio managed to achieve this effect by restricting decoration to the arches that divide up the bays of the nave, the entablature at the base of the barrel vault and dome, and the pediments over the window tabernacles. These are picked out in grey *pietra serena,* offset against the white walls. The details are very fine.

Francesco di Giorgio's building was widely recognized as a masterpiece. It was in a spirit of rivalry that the art historian, painter and architect Vasari attempted to surpass it in the church of Santa Maria Nuova, built fifty years later just beyond the western wall of the town. It stands in a better position than Santa Maria del Calcinaio, and is best seen from above, where its terracotta-coloured dome rises from amid the olives. Unlike Di Giorgio's building, with its longitudinal axis, Vasari's adopted the Greek cross plan, but not totally successfully, since the interior, with its subdued lighting and monumental arches, is a trifle gloomy.

Cortona possesses numerous other delights, although you need to be at your fittest, or have a Fiat Cinquecento handy, to enjoy the more remote churches, set on precipitous streets, or the houses actually built on the old Etruscan walls. If you have the energy, two of Fra Angelico's most beautiful altar-pieces hang in the Museo Diocesano, and the little church of San Niccolò, with its charming walled forecourt and cypresses, possesses a superb Deposition by Signorelli over the altar, which the custodian will delight in detaching from the wall by an electric hinge so that you can admire the Madonna and Child on the reverse. At the summit of the town, the view is quite extraordinary, stretching half-way across Tuscany to Monte Amiata in the far distance.

The three pilgrimage churches in this section sum up the dichotomy of the Quattrocento. One of the most brilliant eras in Italian history, it marks the transition between the medieval and the modern world. The architects who designed these buildings were bursting with new ideas, inspired by the achievements of their contemporaries and the classical world. This was their moment to experiment with the Greek cross design, the most up-to-date architectural plan. And yet the congregations who gathered to worship in these churches were drawn by more primitive emotions. They came to pray to the Virgin and to celebrate the miracles that had occurred here. In the sixteenth century, the Counter-Reformation and the Inquisition swept away many of the humanist achievements of the Renaissance, and the reason that they found it so easy to reintroduce the cult of the saints, particularly the Virgin, was that in Italy as elsewhere people had never really ceased to believe in them.

TOUR 6

ART CONQUERS NATURE

VILLA FARNESE, CAPRAROLA · VILLA LANTE, BAGNAIA · SACRO BOSCO, BOMARZO

The Villa Farnese by Vignola at Caprarola is the most magnificent villa in Italy, with frescoes glorifying the Farnese family. Behind the villa lies a charming secret garden.

Starting-point: Villa Farnese, Caprarola

Recommended time: Full day

Length of tour: 20 miles (34km)

Best time of year: April/May or September/October

Finishing-point: Sacro Bosco, Bomarzo

The three villas and gardens in this section represent the culmination of the Renaissance garden. All lie within a few kilometres of each other near the town of Viterbo, and can be visited within a day. The Villa Farnese has most to see, and you should devote a whole morning or afternoon to it. The three gardens, dating from the second half of the sixteenth century, are contemporary with one another, and were created in a spirit of friendly rivalry. It is therefore all the more fascinating to study the different methods the owners and their architects employed in shaping nature to their own particular designs, using all the tricks of perspective so beloved of the Renaissance to allow each garden to unfold its secrets as the spectator moves through it.

During the Middle Ages, the countryside was somewhere to be avoided. Those few who were prepared to risk living outside towns and villages did so in fortified castles. A garden was either set within a cloister or a walled enclosure, known as the *hortus conclusus*, so lovingly depicted in views of paradise in illuminated manuscripts. This view of nature was challenged, initially by Petrarch, the first man recorded to have climbed a mountain to enjoy the view from the summit, and later, in the early fifteenth century, by Cosimo de' Medici, who used to retire with his humanist friends to his favourite villa of Careggi outside Florence, 'not to cultivate my fields but my soul'. This new idea of the villa, not as a working farm, but as a place to retreat to from the pressures of city life, characterizes all the great villas of Renaissance Rome.

The first of these villas was created in 1504 by Bramante to house Pope Julius II's collection of antique sculpture in the Belvedere Court in the Vatican. Bramante's imposition of symmetry and order on a whole hillside by creating terraces, flanking loggias and ramped staircases, each an autonomous unit, but part of a unified whole, and his setting of statuary against a backdrop of pergolas and grottoes, created an architectural format which was adopted by all the major Roman gardens of the next generation.

This era of lavish architectural patronage was brought to a precipitate halt by the Sack of Rome in 1527. It was not until Spain emerged victorious from its dynastic struggle with France in the middle of the century that the princes of the church felt secure enough to construct villas and gardens on their feudal estates outside Rome. Their favourite architect, Vignola, sought inspiration from Bramante.

Vignola's transformation of the Villa Farnese at Caprarola from a fortress into a villa, or more properly a palace, began in 1555. The building, set on axis at the top of a series of ramped staircases, looks straight back to the Belvedere Court. The villa dominates the surrounding countryside. Cardinal Alessandro Farnese, the greatest patron of the arts of his era, came here to indulge his passion for hunting, during a golden age before the widespread use of firearms destroyed the abundance of game in central Italy. The splendour of the villa reflects the Cardinal's sense of magnificence. The historian Jacob Burckhardt called the villa 'perhaps the highest example of restrained majesty which secular architecture has achieved'.

Cardinal Carlo Borromeo, a champion of the Counter-Reformation, was less than amused by the ostentatious display of wealth, and asked Cardinal Farnese sharply why he did not distribute his riches to the poor, to which the worldly Cardinal, who, as the grandson of Pope Paul III, was not to be put

down by anyone, least of all a nosy fellow cardinal, replied: 'I have given it to them little by little, but I have made them earn it by the sweat of their brows'.

Cardinal Farnese brought with him an army of retainers for his annual summer retreat from the sweltering heat of Rome. The scale of his entertaining was legendary. Although the villa was technically no more than a hunting lodge, it attracted the grandest visitors, including in 1578 Pope Gregory XIII, who was led in by a procession of one hundred maidens in white, bearing olive branches and cymbals. The Cardinal was endlessly competing with his great rival Cardinal Ippolito d'Este, who entered his see at Tivoli in 1550 in a chariot pulled by Moorish slaves.

Vignola's plan for the villa is highly original: a pentagon with a circular courtyard in the middle to let in the light. This shows the influence of Bramante, who also inspired the frescoed spiral staircase. The rooms surrounding the courtyard are divided into summer and winter apartments, facing north and south respectively. This was something that Pliny had recommended in antiquity in his description of his Tuscan villa, and which had already been adopted by Raphael in the Villa Madama, on the outskirts of Rome. The rooms were frescoed with appropriate themes by Taddeo and Federico Zuccaro and their assistants. The summer apartments contained episodes from the life of Hercules (the local god and a great favourite in Renaissance iconography) in the guard room, scenes glorifying the Farnese family in the reception rooms, contemplative subjects in the studies, and mythological scenes suggesting night and sleep in the bedrooms. The winter apartments were frescoed with predominantly religious subjects, better befitting a cardinal. The last of the rooms you visit is the Map Room, containing a comprehensive view of the world as it was known in 1574. Much of the coastline is reasonably accurate, apart from North America, and it is generally the interior of the continents where the imagination of the artists, Giovanni Vanosino da Varese, Giovanni de' Vecchi

and Raffaelino da Reggio, has run riot.

At the back of the villa, connected by a drawbridge over the moat, are two formal gardens with quartered parterres, the winter one planted with flowers set within box and privet hedges, the summer one with fruit trees to provide shade. At the far end Vignola constructed two grottoes, a favourite device in the Renaissance since it allowed for the creation of artificial effects out of nature and for the indulgence of a passion for water jokes. The effect of rain coming through the ceiling particularly impressed Montaigne on his visit in 1581. We are now only capable of visualizing a garden as a place devoted to pleasure, but in the Renaissance it was intended to encompass all sides of life, and the grotto represented the darker side of nature. In Leonardo da Vinci's words, a visitor was meant to experience 'fear of the dark and threatening cave; and a desire to see whether there might be any marvellous thing therein'. Grottoes induced a *frisson* of terror in the visitor, much as we now enjoy the thrill of a horror movie.

Above the formal gardens, a path leads up the hill away from the villa through chestnut and fir trees. A word of warning: the chestnuts are so popular with locals that the garden is closed for a period during September and October so that they can pick the fruit from the ground. Immediately, you are distanced from the villa. Turning right at the corner of the path, a vista opens up to a casino, standing at the head of a flight of steps, where the Cardinal could escape his entourage. It is one of the most surprising, and delightful, prospects in Italy. Approaching a pool, with a water staircase beyond, you are beckoned on by two herms.

The theme of this garden is light-hearted frivolity. The Water Chain, designed, like the other fountains, by the comically named Maccarone, is composed of dolphins, down which the water cascades. Above, a gigantic vase spouts water in the shape of the Farnese lily, flanked by two river gods. The scale of the sculpture is topsy-turvy; the vase completely dwarfs the unicorn standing directly

Previous page: Vignola's Villa Farnese at Caprarola has an unusual pentagonal plan and dominates the view from miles around. The charming formal garden is visible on the left.

behind it. At the top of the steps you suddenly come across a secret garden in front of a casino, probably built by Giacomo del Duca in 1584-7, enclosed by a series of herms by Pietro Bernini, the great baroque sculptor's father (their heads supposedly portraits of the workmen), joking and making music. This favourite picnic spot of the Cardinal is an intimate, silent place, far removed from the magnificence of the villa below. Queen Christina of Sweden summed up its sensual, pagan atmosphere when she wrote: 'I dare not speak the name of Jesus lest I break the spell'. On the far side of the casino, a series of flower-beds, laid out around 1620 by Rainaldi, who also built the rusticated grottoes at the foot of the Water Chain, lead up to a gate beyond which one enters the realm of wild nature.

The Villa Lante is the finest Renaissance garden near Rome. A succession of interconnected fountains runs down the hillside. Two pavilions overlook the lower terrace.

Whereas the garden at Caprarola offers a series of surprises, that at the Villa Lante over-whelms the visitor with sheer delight. It lies 20km north of Caprarola in the village of Bagnaia, 5km east of the ancient papal city of Viterbo. The picturesque road runs through thick oak woods interspersed with fields planted with nut and almond trees. All the experiments carried out on previous Renaissance gardens, with their interaction of art and nature, reach their apogee here. The garden was created out of part of a large hunting park for Cardinal Gambara, the Bishop of Viterbo, probably by Vignola, between 1566 and 1587. In the complexity of its iconographic scheme and in the ingenuity of the treatment of water, it marks an advance on the Villa Farnese.

Although the garden is laid out on axis, architecture, for the first time, is subservient to nature; the two rustic pavilions, the one on the right built by Cardinal Gambara, with frescoes of the Villa Farnese, the Villa d'Este at Tivoli and the Villa Lante itself, the other erected by Cardinal Montalto in 1598, are placed on either side of the main axis, to frame the view. The best viewing-point of the garden contains the usual water jokes which often induce a serious

sense of humour failure in the earnest sightseer, his camera in hand.

It is possible to read the garden on two parallel levels. The one favoured by most art historians is to trace a development from the top to the bottom as nature is gradually tamed by man. From the Fountain of the Deluge, which appears as part of the surrounding countryside, you progress past the Fountain of the Dolphins, representing untamed creatures, to the Water Chain, with its pun on Gambara (crayfish in Italian). You then move down to the Fountain of the River Gods, which introduces a classical element, before passing the Stone Dining Table, inspired by Pliny's description of his villa, and the Fountain of Lights, showing the hallmarks of civilization. The tour ends on the lower terrace with the Fountain of Moors, attributed to Taddeo Landini, holding aloft the Montalto star, set on an island, where man's influence is paramount, and which looks back to the Maritime Theatre at Hadrian's villa at Tivoli.

This analysis should be considered in conjunction with Vignola's masterly treatment of water, the supreme ornament of nature, bringing life, sound and movement into the garden. Water cascades out of the hillside, and rises in the Fountain of the Dolphins before rushing down the Water Chain, varying in sound as it runs between the claws of the crayfish, and over the shells at the bottom of the runnels. It splashes into the Fountain of the River Gods, and flows through the middle of the Dining Table and down into the Fountain of Lights, with its tinkling jets of water, before descending to the placid pool on the lower terrace set in the centre of a box parterre. The Cardinal loved to wander through his garden, and to dine alfresco in the shade of the plane trees, his bottles of Frascati chilled to perfection in the running water.

The water varies both in sound and in the way that it catches the light. The beauty of the reflected light is constantly underestimated by those northerners who have felt inspired to copy aspects of the Italian garden, since water only sparkles in strong

Right: The Fountain of
Pegasus at the Villa Lante
pictured with one of the
casinos beyond.

**The Sacro Bosco at
Bomarzo is a
fascinating garden, full
of monstrous
sculptures. It possesses
a creepy atmosphere.**

sunlight, just as the smell of box hedges is always more intense in a Mediterranean climate, and the shadow they cast more profound. It was this unifying theme of water that Cardinal Aldobrandini was determined to surpass when he began the Villa Aldobrandini at Frascati, the first great baroque garden.

In its human scale, its symmetry and the way in which, in Stendhal's delightful expression, 'the architecture is wedded to the trees', the villa, as Montaigne noted in 1581, surpasses even the Villa d'Este at Tivoli. There is a fascinating theory that Claude Lorraine, heading for Rome in the early seventeenth century, worked in Cardinal Montalto's recently built casino, and one can imagine the impact that the

beauty of the garden made on his impressionable mind, already dreaming of painting the Arcadian landscapes which were, in turn, to exert such an influence on the English landscape garden.

The final garden on this itinerary, 14km north-east of Bagnaia, possesses a bizarre quality which appeals strongly to our era, and particularly fascinated Salvador Dali, who rediscovered it in the 1950s. The Sacro Bosco at Bomarzo is a fascinating place, even though it has been sadly municipalized. Laid out intermittently between 1552 and 1585 by the nobleman-soldier Duke Vicino Orsini, it demonstrates the Mannerist love of obscure allegorical con-

Right: This giant tearing a man apart is one of the disturbing sculptures dotted around the Sacro Bosco at Bomarzo. Top: A fierce dragon confronts the visitor. Bottom: Legend has it that this cave in the shape of a monstrous fish's mouth was the scene of black masses.

ceits, with references to Ariosto's *Orlando Furioso*, and to the many Etruscan monuments in this part of Italy.

The garden should be regarded as a voyage towards self-knowledge, from the lower part, representing base ignorance, to the upper level, symbolizing Arcadia. Some of the sculptures carved out of the rock, such as the Giant tearing a man apart, are truly terrifying. Others, such as the Leaning House, which induces a real feeling of vertigo, are quirky, whereas the cave, whose entrance is shaped like a monstrous mask, with a stone table inside suggesting a pagan altar, is altogether more sinister. It is a measure of the power of these stone statues that an official exorcism was performed in the park in 1980. It is with a feeling

of relief that one reaches the Hippodrome above, lined with giant urns, acorns and pine cones, representing a Golden Age. At the highest point, Orsini commissioned Vignola to build a simple but elegant temple in memory of his wife Giulia.

Despite the classical and literary associations, Orsini seems to be mocking the Renaissance principles of harmony and order and laughing at the pretensions of those who believe in them. He described the garden as 'one of those castles of Atlantis where paladins and ladies are held by careless enchantments'. It is a place of magic, full of snares and spells designed to test the visitor as hero as he searches for his goal.

ETRUSCAN MYSTERIES

MONTEMERANO · SOVANA · SORANO · PITIGLIANO · TARQUINIA · VULCI

Montemerano is a picturesque village with some interesting works of art in the church of San Giorgio.

The Etruscans remain an elusive and mysterious race who flit across the pages of history. No literature survives, their historical records are indecipherable, and few champions have stepped forward to defend their position as the most intransigent opponents of Rome. Even in antiquity the memory of the Etruscans had disappeared into an obscurity as dark as the sepulchral gloom of their tombs. Nothing remains but the glory of their art, and the thought that perhaps it is to them, rather than the dour Romans of the Republic, that the modern Italian owes his extrovert charm, his wit, his natural elegance and his ability to laugh at himself.

Perched on strategic hilltops, the towns of the Etruscan Confederation formed the main barrier to the expanding power of Rome. The conflict between the two races was so long and bloody that the Romans did their utmost to obliterate the Etruscan civilization by depopulating their cities, razing their buildings to the ground and suppressing their culture. This elusive quality appealed greatly to the Romantics, and makes the search for their identity all the more fascinating and tantalizing.

Etruria encompasses the centre of Italy, extending from the Apennines to the western coast, and from Bologna and northern Tuscany to the outskirts of Rome. It was never a country, but a loose federation of city-states united by race and religious rites. From humble beginnings in the ninth century BC, the Etruscans rapidly became a prosperous farming and seafaring people, trading all over Italy and throughout the Mediterranean. They benefited greatly from contact with the Greek colonies in southern Italy, and were producing works of the highest artistic quality by the seventh and sixth centuries BC. After 474BC, when the Etruscan navy was annihilated by the

Cumaeans and Syracusans, their coastal towns declined, and they turned to agriculture and exploited mineral deposits of copper, tin, lead and iron ore. The struggle to contain the Romans, immortalized in Macaulay's *Lays of Ancient Rome*, intensified in the fourth century, and ended with the Etruscan cities being forced to sign a humiliating series of treaties with the new superpower in Italy in the third century.

However, much survives from their heyday, and many of the most interesting Etruscan settlements are congregated on the border of Tuscany and Lazio. Here you can study the rich artistic talent of the Etruscans, and the way in which they learnt from the Greeks and, in turn, inspired the Romans. The sites in this section should, ideally, be seen from a base in one of the resorts on the coast, such as Porto Santo Stefano, Porto Ercole or Orbetello on the Monte Argentario peninsula. I have divided the section into two parts, the first devoted to an exploration of the landscape of Etruria, the second to two of the most important Etruscan sites, both of which possess excellent museums.

If you are starting from Monte Argentario, take the Via Aurelia north for 10km and head inland on the SS74 from Albinia. This is one of the most beautiful roads in central Italy and passes through a number of Etruscan towns. For the initial 33km to Manciano, the road rises steadily from sea level, at first flanked by umbrella pines and cypresses, which gradually give way to vines and cornfields, with a smattering of oaks, which, in turn, are replaced by thick oak woods interspersed with the occasional olive grove. The view back from Manciano towards the coast is particularly impressive, the silvery green of the olives standing out against the red earth.

Starting-point: Monte Argentario

Recommended time: A day and a half

Length of tour: 63 miles (102km) + 17 miles (27km) for Tarquinia and Vulci

Best time of year: April/May or September/October

Finishing-point: Vulci

From Manciano turn left, and after 6km you will come to Montemerano, a picturesque village sitting on a hilltop. Little disturbs the calm here, apart from the occasional cock crowing, or a tractor and trailer emerging from an impossibly narrow alley. The Romanesque church of San Giorgio, for once tastefully redecorated in the baroque style, is, rather surprisingly, full of Renaissance frescoes and sculpture. Some of the leading Sienese artists worked here, and somehow Sano di Pietro's polyptych of the Madonna and Child with Saints, and Vecchietta's slightly cross-eyed statue of St Peter, both dating from the mid-fifteenth century, appear more at home than if they were sitting neglected in the basement of a museum in Siena.

Beyond Montemerano, continue north towards the slopes of Monte Amiata, the highest mountain in southern Tuscany. A quick detour to Saturnia, after 6km, will suffice to take in the Etruscan walls and the Roman gate. The landscape gradually unfolds as the road continues to climb. After 9km, turn right to San Martino sul Fiora, where a vast panorama to the south and the east over the whole of southern Etruria spreads out at your feet, one of the most spectacular views in central Italy. You now gradually descend for 10km until you reach Sovana.

Sovana is a very pretty village with two good Romanesque churches, one with a beautiful ciborium. Outside the village are some ancient Etruscan rock-cut tombs.

Just outside the town, you pass two parts of an ancient Etruscan necropolis. They are not the best known in Etruria, but possess a stronger atmosphere than many more famous sites, and capture something of the mystery of this civilization. The necropolis of Poggio Prisca, on the left of the valley, with its impressive early third-century Tomb of Hildebrand (named in honour of the great medieval Pope Gregory VII, who was born in Sovana) is the more complete, but it has none of the haunting quality of the Tomb of the Siren, on the right side of the road beyond the stream. The tomb stands on the north side of the valley in thick woodland, above an overgrown path. With the sun slanting through the beeches and chestnuts, and wild cyclamen scattered at your feet, there is a touch of real magic to this place. The path becomes increasingly overgrown, and the tombs are hacked more haphazardly from the rock face, sometimes even appearing to be cut beneath it. A narrow gulley leads up to the left, with a slightly sinister atmosphere, as though the souls of the Etruscans buried here may have left behind something of their presence.

Sovana itself it one of the prettiest towns in Etruria. Its small size means that you are constantly catching glimpses down side streets into the surrounding countryside. The Duomo stands outside the town and is approached by a cobbled road between rows of vines. The spacious interior, dating from the eleventh and twelfth centuries, is very impressive, although the arches supporting the crossing look in imminent danger of collapse. The north door contains some good carving, particularly the comical knight seated on his horse, a primitive Don Quixote, his legs trailing almost down to the ground, and waving his sword to show that he means business.

Sovana's piazza is no more than an expansion of the main street. A number of small palaces face on to the square, including the Palazzo Pretoria, its façade encrusted with coats of arms, and the Palazzetto dell' Archivio, which appears as a tower adorned with a campanile.

The Romanesque church of Santa Maria flanks the piazza, decorated with a number of fifteenth-century frescoes, including a damaged Annunciation and a Madonna and Child with Saints, where St Lucy's eyes, sitting in a bowl, stare out disconcertingly at the spectator. The gem of the church, and one of the masterpieces of the Dark Ages, is the ciborium, dating from the eighth or ninth century. The exquisite carving, a mixture of geometric decoration and vines, and the intricacy of the capitals, emphasize the importance of Sovana in the early Middle Ages, when it ruled southern Etruria.

Sovana is scarcely larger than a village. But, set in a remote, rural landscape it sums up the charm of the Maremma: the forgotten province of Tuscany.

Opposite: The houses of the Etruscan town of Sorano cling to the side of a gorge. Top: The Etruscan Tomb of the Siren, carved from the rock, emerges from the woods in the valley below Sovana. Bottom: The dramatic first century BC Ponte della Badia spans the ravine beside the castle of Vulci.

The approach to Sovana, via a tunnel cut through the rock, is dramatic enough, but nothing like as spectacular as that to its neighbours Sorano and Pitigliano. Lying some 10km to the north-east and south-east respectively, both towns are sited for defensive purposes on the lips of gorges. There can be no clearer indication of the importance of strategic considerations. The houses at the top of Sorano seem to rise sheer out of the cliff face, and this, together with the endless stairways, the entrances to houses on bridges straddling streets, and the views down to the tombs at the foot of the gorge, induce a feeling of vertigo in the visitor. Sadly, many of the houses are in ruins behind their impressive rusticated doorways – a reminder that what appears picturesque to the tourist often indicates dire poverty for the locals.

Pitigliano is possibly in an even better position, at the junction of two gorges. This was once a stronghold of the Orsini, one of the two leading families of medieval Rome, and even the street names (Vicolo del Tiranno and Vicolo della Battiglia) testify to its warlike past. The town is grander than Sorano, and filled with palaces, clustered near the overpowering Orsini fortress. It is also a lot more prosperous, and many of the houses have been converted into shops selling furniture.

This route, deep into the heart of Etruria, captures the charm of the countryside which brought the Etruscans their wealth. The rest of this section is devoted to Tarquinia and Vulci, both important settlements near the coast. Unless you wish to visit them immediately, you might like to continue on the SS74 in a leisurely fashion and enjoy the beauty of Lake Bolsena, and later devote a complete day to their necropolises and museums.

Tarquinia is a major Etruscan site, and was probably head of the Etruscan Confederation that fought so long and hard against Rome. The objects in the museum bring to life the sophisticated culture of this area. Even if you have seen the Villa Giulia in Rome, or the Archaeological Museum in Florence, it is still well worth admiring the excellent selection of sarcophagi and pots in the Museo Nazionale Tarquiniense, housed in the handsome Palazzo Vitelleschi. The best of these date from the sixth to the fourth century BC, and rival in quality the sculpture and ceramics of classical Greece.

The figures reclining on the lids of the sarcophagi are particularly lifelike: Partunu with his paunch sagging over the edge of the lid, and a magistrate resting his head on his left hand as though deliberating evidence. Upstairs, the black figures on the red vases display the artists' mastery in portraying movement, as the figures run and fight with complete freedom. Like the Greeks, whose art forms theirs so resemble, the Etruscans were equally at home depicting warriors fighting, religious rites – especially Dionysiac dances – feasts with slaves making music, or love-making.

In the room to the left of the staircase, two winged horses, taken from the so-called altar of the Queen where they originally decorated the front of a temple, stand proudly against the wall. It seems fitting that they should have come from the Great House of Tarquin. And indeed these graceful animals are linked to Tarquinia's great struggle with Rome, for it was probably on the altar of this temple, in 358BC, that 307 Roman prisoners were sacrificed. For the Etruscans, as for the Romans, beauty and cruelty were inextricably intertwined.

Tarquinia also possesses a fascinating necropolis, but before you visit the painted tombs, you should not miss some of the town's medieval architecture. The finest building is the church of Santa Maria di Castello, which lies just outside the impressive Porta Castello, on the west side of the town. The bare façade, with traces of Cosmatesque decoration around the central window and door, gives little indication of the superb twelfth-century interior. It stands in the shadow of a soaring tower – one of several which give Tarquinia its distinctive skyline.

As so often with the best Romanesque architecture, its beauty lies in its uncluttered simplicity, with unornamented walls, and no colour to detract from the pale yellow limestone apart from the porphyry and *verde antica* of the Cosmatesque pavement. Both the patrons and the artists took great pride in their work here. An inscription states that Prior Orso erected the ciborium in 1168, and it is worth quoting in full the proud inscription on the pulpit: *Nel nome del Signore, cosi sia l'anno 1206, indizione XI, nel mese di Agosto, in tempo di Papa Innocenzo III, io Angelo Priore di questa chiesa feci fare questo lavoro, splendido di oro e marmi diversi, per le mani di Maestro Giovanni figlio di Guittone cittadino Romano.* (In the name of the lord, in the year 1206, in the month of August, in the reign of Pope Innocent III, I, Angelo, Prior of this church, commissioned this work, resplendent with gold and different marbles, from the hand of Master Giovanni, son of Guittone, a Roman citizen.)

The Etruscan necropolis, lying 2km outside Tarquinia on the road to Viterbo, is one of the most important in existence because of the quality of its painted tombs. Interest in them stretches back to the eighteenth century, when the Grand Tourist and canny art dealer Thomas Jenkins began excavating here. The site itself is rather disappointing, with gnomic huts with sloping roofs fenced in by wire, but, once you descend underground, you are transported back in time. The paintings, with their brilliant reds and blacks, and their athletic figures and animals, give a vivid idea of the Etruscan love of feasting, competing in funereal games, hunting, and fighting. The best of them date from the sixth and fifth centuries BC. Aesthetically, it is a tragedy that the Etruscans were defeated, since these paintings, together with the sculpture and pottery in the museum, are far in advance of anything that the Romans were capable of producing at that time.

Those who feel that, fascinating though the Etruscans undoubtedly are, enough is enough, might like to continue from the necropolis to Tuscania, whose two Romanesque churches of San Pietro and Santa Maria Maggiore rival Santa Maria di Castello in

their beauty and the quality of their carving. Those eager to understand better how the Etruscans actually lived, on the other hand, can make a short diversion at Montalto di Castro, on the road back to Orbetello, to the black, forbidding castle at Vulci.

Once the seat of Cardinal Alessandro Farnese, the grandson of Pope Paul III and builder of Caprarola (see page 43), the castle now houses a fascinating collection of artefacts from the Etruscan site, first discovered when Lucien Buonaparte lived here in 1828. The finds range from *bucchero* pots (made of a local black ceramic), highly decorated amphorae, images of household deities, often associated with the cult of Apollo, and carvings of bulls' heads. Although these objects vary in quality, the fact that they were all excavated here conveys the lifestyle of the Etruscans more vividly than many a more important collection.

Next to the castle stands the imposing Ponte della Badia, built in the local tufa, in the first century BC. Its high arch still spans the ravine as firmly as the day it was completed. The site of Vulci itself, despite its size and importance, and the wealth of material excavated, is very ruinous, and is best left to the local inhabitants, a fact acknowledged on the archaeological notice: *Attenzione – Pericolo Vipere.*

The forbidding castle of Vulci possesses a good Etruscan museum. Beside the castle stands an impressive bridge two thousand years old.

THE VENETO
AND FRIULI

More than anywhere else in Italy, the charm of the Veneto lies principally in its art. The astonishing concentration of superb villas, the extraordinary number of important artists born in the province and the artistic heritage of the main towns, provide a constant source of fascination. Wherever you travel, from the hills of the north to the low-lying plain south of Padua and Vicenza, your eye is drawn to the fine buildings that line the roads and canals, and to the fortified towns that rise up on the horizon.

The Veneto's history is closely reflected in its art. For many centuries the Veneto and its neighbour Friuli have been united in a single entity, at first under the sway of Rome and later under the hegemony of Venice. During both these periods the all-pervasive artistic influence was that of classicism. In antiquity the north-eastern corner of the Italian peninsula was noted chiefly as the birthplace of Ovid, Livy and Virgil. During the thousand years of the Byzantine Empire, long after Rome herself had fallen, the towns and ports of the Adriatic coast maintained their links with Constantinople and the East. This is evident in the wonderful churches in Friuli erected at Aquileia and Grado, decorated with glittering mosaics.

In the Veneto itself the classical influence declined in the Middle Ages, as the fiercely independent city states of Padua, Treviso, Verona and Vicenza adopted the Gothic style for their most important civic and religious buildings. But classicism never entirely died away, and it was at Arqua Petrarca in the Euganean Hills of the Veneto, that Petrarch, one of the first humanists and the precursor of the Renaissance, spent the last years of his life. Petrarch's sojourn at Arqua Petrarca coincided with the gradual conquest of the region by Venice who was anxious to expand her land holdings, and eager to take over the lucrative trade routes to Milan and over the Alps to the Holy Roman Empire.

The Renaissance originated in Florence, but two of the leading Quattrocento artists came to the Veneto to execute many of their major works. The sculptor Donatello and the painter Mantegna were both enthusiastic champions of the study of Roman art. It was largely due to their influence, and in particular to that of Mantegna whose brother-in-law was Giovanni Bellini, that the Renaissance entered Venice. The architects of the Veneto were slower than their contemporaries elsewhere in Italy to adopt the classical style. They more than made up for this hesitation with the figure of Andrea Palladio, the Renaissance architect from Padua, most closely imbued with the spirit of the classical world.

Two centuries later Canova was born in the little town of Possagno in the north of the province. He was an extraordinarily successful sculptor of Neo-classicism – a style that was a second deliberate evocation of antiquity. Even Tiepolo, the last major Venetian painter, and an artist famous for his luscious naked figures soaring effortlessly across vast expanses of ceiling, devoted most of his career to painting classical subjects.

The most logical base from which to visit the province, and for four of the itineraries I have chosen, is Vicenza, an architectural student's dream. Although the neighbouring cities of Padua and Verona possess more classical associations and remains, Vicenza appears like a Renaissance vision of antiquity. Palladio's handsome palaces dominate every street and piazza. From the façade of the Basilica, which encloses the medieval town hall like a giant tea cosy, to the Teatro Olimpico, with its extraordinary recreation of the city of Thebes (as Palladio imagined it), you can trace the architect's entire career. A short walk outside the town to the south-east takes you to the Villa Rotonda, the most influential of all his villas. You can make any number of additional excursions along the canals and back roads to the villas that dot the surrounding countryside.

Vicenza stands on the edge of the Veneto's most beautiful countryside. At first the landscape is predominantly flat, with avenues of poplars casting lengthening shadows across dusty roads. But gradually the countryside rises to the Dolomites. The inhabitants of this northern part of the province are mountain people, the prosperous middle classes dressed in loden coats, the labourers dropping in at their local bar for a fortifying glass of grappa on their way to work. I have avoided the main towns and concentrated instead on places which are difficult to reach without a car. It is all too easy to get lost. Much of the Veneto has, sadly, become rather built up, and one village tends to merge with another, so that signposts can be most misleading. Remember that Frazione refers to a district, not an actual village, and you will save yourself many a tortured argument over map reading. Wherever you are, you will drive past a wealth of beautiful architecture, so that there is no need to rush your sightseeing, which is always a recipe for disaster. Hurrying through the smaller towns and villages gives you little chance to enjoy some of the most memorable images of the Veneto: evening mist shrouding a Palladian villa guarded by a phalanx of dilapidated statues, swifts darting round the ivy-clad crenellations of a ruined tower, and a team of Venetian gondoliers, fresh from victory in a Regatta, rowing lazily up the Brenta canal.

Friuli, the province adjoining the Veneto to the north-east, is most famous for its delicious fruity white wine, which far surpasses anything produced by the better-known Soave or Valpolicella. The locals take a keen interest in their wine, and if you ever have the luck to stay in a Venetian palace in September, you will notice the servants casting an anxious eye to the heavens as they prepare to set off for the *vendemmia*, or wine harvest. You can visit Aquileia, the province's masterpiece, either on an excursion from Venice, or from Udine, which will allow you to admire this handsome but virtually unknown town, where some of the finest frescoes by the young Giambattista Tiepolo can be seen in the Archbishop's Palace.

Opposite: The Tempietto at Maser is Palladio's last masterpiece: a delightful recreation of the Pantheon in Rome. Left: The garden of the Istituto Filippino in Asolo demonstrates the charm of this small hill-town, a great favourite with all visitors.

PALLADIAN PAGEANT

VILLA EMO, FANZOLO · ASOLO · VILLA BARBARO, MASER

The Villa Emo is one of Palladio's most successful designs. The handsome central block was used as a farmhouse by the Emo family, with the two side wings as storehouses.

Starting-point: Villa Emo, Fanzolo

Recommended time: Short day

Length of tour: 16 miles (26km)

Best time of year: May/June or September/October

Finishing-point: Villa Barbaro, Maser

The flat, fertile countryside of the Veneto possesses an unparalleled collection of villas dating back to the Renaissance. In the fifteenth century, with the decline of her overseas trade following Vasco da Gama's exploration of the sea route to India, and Columbus's discovery of America, and the drain on her resources from the endless war with the mighty Turkish empire, Venice expanded her territorial holdings on the Italian mainland. The Venetian nobility, enriched by centuries of lucrative trade with the Orient, and emboldened by Venice's rapid success in regaining her possessions following the horrors of the War of the League of Cambrai at the beginning of the sixteenth century, began to drain the marshes and cultivate the rich farmland of their country estates. During the course of the century, villas sprang up all over the Veneto, and, in answer to this demand, an architect appeared whose ideas on villa design were to prove the most original and influential in Italian history.

Andrea di Pietro (1508-80), nicknamed Palladio in honour of Pallas Athene, the Greek goddess of wisdom, rose from being a humble stonemason from Padua to become the favourite architect of Venice's golden age, and a prolific designer of villas, churches and palaces. His villas, which were to be so enormously influential, show distinctive characteristics: harmonious proportions, symmetrical planning, and the application of the classical temple front to the façade (since Roman temples were thought, wrongly, to derive from domestic buildings). These features served his patrons well; imbued with the world of antiquity, of which there were ample remains in this corner of Italy, Venetian nobles applied the concept of *otium*, or pleasure, as described by the Roman writer Pliny the Younger in his letters, to

working farms. The villas were predominantly used during harvest-time, when the patricians came out from the cities to inspect their crops. I have chosen two of the finest Palladian villas, situated towards the Dolomites in the north of the province. Both contrast a relatively simple exterior with a lavish interior.

The Villa Emo at Fanzolo lies just north of the SS53, which runs between Vicenza and Treviso. Turn left at Vedelago, 7km beyond Castelfranco. Built between 1555 and 1565, the villa represents one of the most satisfactory solutions to the problem of creating a building with both a domestic and an agricultural purpose. A simple raised central section, designed as a temple front with Tuscan Doric columns, is approached by a long ramp, on which corn was threshed, and up which the owner rode to his front door. The Emos still own the villa, and can watch the harvest from the windows, and smell the scent of new-mown hay in the fields, just as they have done for centuries.

On either side of the central block, two long *barchesse*, or arcaded wings, with their alternating rhythm of light and shade, provide store-rooms. They testify to the wealth of Leonardo di Alvise Emo, a shrewd farmer who introduced the highly profitable maize crop on his estate. Two dovecotes at either end of the wings provide vertical accents to counter the predominant horizontal emphasis, as does the avenue of poplars leading up to the villa. Don't take too seriously the idea that the pigeons in the dovecotes were used to keep Emo in communication with events in Venice; they were more likely to end up in his stomach than bring him news from the Rialto. The beauty of the Villa Emo lies in the union of the restrained central building with the two handsome wings, the understatement of Palladio's design, and the integration of the whole with the landscape.

The interior is considerably more elaborate, the walls covered in frescoes painted by Veronese's pupil Zelotti between 1560 and 1565. They are devoted to humanistic ideals: the arts, classical myths, justice, and virtue, epitomized by the 'Continence of Scipio' in the main hall. The figures of Turkish prisoners beneath the fresco were a topical inclusion, since they were painted just before the great naval victory over the Turks at the battle of Lepanto in 1571, in which the Venetians played a crucial part. Zelotti's frescoes are good examples of their kind, but they pale into insignificance when compared with the work of Veronese at the Villa Barbaro at Maser.

B efore going to Maser, you might like to stop at Asolo, the prettiest hill-town in the Veneto. From Fanzolo, head north to Caselle, bear left at Altivole, and follow the signs straight on to Asolo. Despite the influx of foreigners and the *beau monde* enjoying the luxuries of the Cipriani Hotel, the town has retained its charm. Writers seem particularly susceptible to the beauty of the place. Browning fell head over heels in love with Asolo on his first visit to Italy in 1838, and Freya Stark, one of the greatest contemporary travel writers, was born here (within 50 metres of Browning's house). She built herself a magical villa on the outskirts of the town, and dining alfresco in the loggia on summer evenings, with the lights beginning to twinkle in the plain beneath, provided an unforgettable experience for her guests.

Asolo first came to prominence when it was given to Queen Caterina Cornaro in exchange for Cyprus. The unfortunate Caterina, a pawn in the grand game of European diplomacy, at which the wily Venetians excelled, contented herself with creating a model Renaissance court, presided over by Cardinal Bembo. They idled away their time, composing poems, playing literary games and dreaming of past glories, from which the verb *asolare* (to idle away time in a frivolous fashion) derives. Caterina's castle still survives, perched above the town. While

in the town, do not miss the powerful Lorenzo Lotto altar-piece of the Madonna with Saints Basilio and Antonio in the church on the piazza.

A fter a good lunch in Asolo, perhaps sampling the delectable *tagliatelle verde* in the Cipriani (if you can afford it), you will be ready to tackle the most enjoyable of all Palladio's villas. The Villa Barbaro stands in the little village of Maser, some 5km east of Asolo. Set in more rural landscape than the Villa Emo, at the foot of the Dolomites, it has a similar, though more elaborate, division between the prominent central temple front and the side arcades, ending in dovecotes, decorated with sundials. The temple front, adorned with the Barbaro coat of arms to emphasize the owners' importance, probably derives from the temple of Fortuna Virilis in Rome. The raised loggia on the *piano nobile*, set within the temple front, affords an excellent view of the landscape. The villa was erected between 1549 and 1558 for Daniele and Marc Antonio Barbaro, making it almost exactly contemporary with the Villa Emo.

However, the villa's full glory is only revealed in the interior. Ironically, despite the harmonious proportions of the rooms, this is not due to Palladio at all, but to Veronese, the greatest fresco painter of Venice's golden age. This may account for the way that Palladio, perhaps in a fit of pique, omitted all reference to Veronese's work here in his *Quattro Libri*.

Between 1560 and 1562 Veronese covered the walls of the interior with a series of illusionistic frescoes of the gods and goddesses of antiquity, members of the Barbaro family, and delightful landscapes filled with classical ruins. The Barbaro brothers approved of this scheme of decoration. Daniele was the rector of Padua university, famed for its classical studies, had already edited and translated a version of Vitruvius's *De Architectura*, and was Patriarch elect of Aquileia, with its wealth of classical remains. Marc Antonio had served as a highly distinguished Venetian ambassador to France and Constantinople, and had been appointed Procurator of Venice for life, the

Asolo is a beautiful hill-town on the edge of the Dolomites. It has captivated all visitors and inhabitants, including Robert Browning and Freya Stark.

The Villa Barbaro was built by Palladio and frescoed by Veronese. It is one of the great masterpieces of the golden age of Venetian art.

Above: A bravura self-portrait of Veronese returning from hunting.
Opposite: Marc Antonio Barbaro's wife Giustiniana, her nurse and pet spaniel gaze over the balustrade into the hall of the Villa Barbaro.

characters intrude into this charmed world. A long enfilade bisects the villa; at one end a huntsman, thought to be Veronese himself, enters through a *trompe-l'oeil* door, while his wife, or more probably his mistress, waits to greet him at the other end. In the hall, Marc Antonio Barbaro's wife Giustiniana, in her elegant dress, accompanied by her nurse and a little spaniel, gazes down over a fictive balustrade. The landscapes are designed to increase the illusion that the spectator is looking at the surrounding countryside, visible out of the windows, conjuring up an Arcadian idyll.

The frescoed rooms are set on the *piano nobile*, allowing the visitor a good view over the Barbaro estate. At the back of the *piano nobile*, the Sala dell' Olimpia leads straight out into the *nymphaeum*. This *nymphaeum*, a cool oasis in summer, was fed by a spring which irrigates the garden, before filling two drinking troughs on the main road. The classical statues around the pool and grotto are probably the work of Alessandro Vittoria, and are a direct reference to the great Renaissance villas in Rome, such as the Villa Giulia.

All the artists working on the villa understood the Barbaros' passion for antiquity. Both Veronese and Vittoria had already worked for Daniele Barbaro in the Palazzo Trevisan on the island of Murano, and Palladio may have accompanied his future patron to Rome in 1554. If so, the journey bore rich fruit in the exquisite little chapel he built in 1579-80, one of his last works. This is one of the most charming and intimate copies of the Pantheon, given a rustic air by its swags of fruit hanging between the columns. It reflects Palladio's deep feeling for ancient Roman architecture and his admiration of Bramante's Tempietto, the only modern building, apart from his own, which he included in his *Quattro Libri*.

The work of Palladio, Veronese and Vittoria at Maser is one of the most successful artistic creations of the entire Renaissance, and fulfils Daniele's ambition to rival 'the true beauty and grace of the Ancients'.

second highest rank in the Venetian Republic.

How often must the two Barbaro brothers, hurrying about their onerous duties in the crowded streets of Venice, have dreamt of escaping to their country estate? They came to the villa to relax and wanted the decoration of the rooms to be suitably light-hearted. Accordingly, Veronese portrayed a hedonistic pagan world, where Venus presides over the loves of Olympus, and Bacchus enjoys the sybaritic pleasures of the *vendemmia*. Contemporary

ARTISTS AT HOME

GIORGIONE · BASSANO · CANOVA

The works of Giorgione, the first Venetian painter of the High Renaissance, are very rare. The Castelfranco altar-piece is one of his most important paintings.

The Venetian school of painters combined a sensual delight in the pictorial effects of colour and light with an interest in realism. The former demonstrates the Venetian love of opulence and their responses to the pellucid quality of light in the Venetian lagoon, while the latter, which led to the development of landscape and genre painting, reflects the fact that so many of the leading painters did not come from the city of Venice, but from the rural hinterland of the Veneto. The development of both landscape and genre painting stems from these artists' love of their native countryside. The golden age of Venetian painting begins with Cima (from Conegliano), Bellini and Carpaccio in the late Quattrocento, continues with Giorgione and Titian (both from the Veneto) during the High Renaissance, and ends with Veronese (from Verona), Jacopo Bassano (from Bassano) and Tintoretto in the second half of the sixteenth century.

The most enigmatic and fascinating of all these artists is Giorgione (c.1478-1510), about whom little is known and whose personality remains elusive to this day. All that we know for certain is that Giorgio Barbarelli came from Castelfranco, a small town, ringed with medieval fortifications, 35km north-east of Vicenza on the SS53. He was nicknamed Giorgione (Big George) – on account of his moral and intellectual stature as much as his physical size – was a great womanizer, and played the lute beautifully.

The dreamy mood he captures in his paintings influenced all who saw them, including the aging Giovanni Bellini, then at the height of his powers, and the emerging Titian. Giorgione died tragically young, of the plague, in 1510, but so strong was his influence that even the forceful Titian took a

further decade to progress beyond his poetic style.

Giorgione's 'Madonna and Child with St Francis and St Liberalis', painted c.1504, hangs in a side chapel of the cold, neoclassical Duomo (dedicated to St Liberalis) in the picturesque walled town of Castelfranco. Like so many of the artist's paintings, the altar-piece's striking effect dwells in the ambivalence between the realistic way in which Giorgione has depicted the figures and the landscape, and the dream world they inhabit. The three figures, arranged in a steep pyramidal composition, appear to be unaware of each other, wrapped in their own thoughts. At the apex of the pyramid, the Madonna is raised far above the two saints on a throne with two high steps that no mere mortal could hope to climb.

The ambiguities do not end here. The perspective of the foreground and the background do not coincide, which increases this elusive quality. All sorts of theories have been advanced to explain what is going on. I have heard an eminent professor argue that the two saints flanking the Madonna are portraits of members of the family that commissioned the painting. This appears to be a rather optimistic argument and it seems much more likely that they are merely idealistic images of the saints.

The joy of Giorgione's paintings is that you can advance whatever theory you like, since it is almost impossible categorically to prove or disprove it. Indeed Vasari, writing within fifty years of Giorgione's death, confessed himself baffled by the Venetian's paintings, as was everyone he questioned, and wrote: 'Heaven knows what it all means.'

Before leaving Castelfranco, glance at the façade of the so-called 'House of Giorgione', right beside the Duomo, with its frescoes of the liberal arts on the façade.

Starting-point: Castelfranco
Recommended time:
Short day
Length of tour: 26 miles
(42km)
Best time of year: May/June
or September/October
Finishing-point: Possagno

Jacopo Bassano is the last major painter of Venice's golden age. His best works in Bassano rank with those of his more famous contemporaries Tintoretto and Veronese.

If Giorgione epitomizes an idealized world, where the figures move, trance-like, through an Arcadian landscape, Jacopo da Ponte, known as Jacopo Bassano (1510-92), born in the year of Giorgione's death, was a more down-to-earth figure. Like all the greatest Venetian artists, he was a superb colourist. He was also typically Venetian in being part of a family industry. Jacopo's two sons, Francesco and Leandro, were both competent and prolific artists, though their work is very uneven and rarely matches that of their father. You can gain a good idea of the quality of Jacopo's best work, and of the wide range of influences on his style, by visiting the Museo Civico in his home town of Bassano. From Castelfranco head back to Cittadella, yet another medieval fortified town, Padua's answer to Treviso's Castelfranco, turn right on the SS47 and continue for 12km to Bassano, a town of arcaded squares and a handsome covered bridge, built to withstand the elements. When the weather is fine, there are magnificent views towards the mountains, a constant inspiration for the Bassanos' landscape painting.

The museum, on the main piazza, possesses paintings from every stage of Jacopo's career. At first he adopted a more prosaic version of Giorgione's poetic idyll, as in the 'Flight into Egypt' of 1534, where St Joseph leads the Virgin and Child on a donkey through a beautiful landscape with a distant view of his native Monte Grappa, the home of the fiery liqueur of that name. After experimenting with a Mannerist love of elongated figures, complex poses and brilliant, surreal colours, at times anticipating the paintings of El Greco, who studied in Venice before leaving for Spain, Bassano reverted to more pastoral subjects with which he felt most at home.

His 'Adoration of the Shepherds with St Victor and St Corona', dating from 1568, shows his affinity with animals and peasants, who are depicted with complete naturalness, even to their dirty feet. Bassano's originality lies in the realism of these genre details, painted with a wealth of incidental detail, and in his bold experimentation with light effects, as in 'St

Martin and the Beggar with St Antony Abbot' of c.1578, where the saint, in his shimmering armour, and the beggar in his red rags, emerge from the smoky twilight. Both these aspects of his painting were to be taken up and developed by Caravaggio and proved immensely influential on seventeenth-century European painting, thus belying Bassano's provincial reputation.

As well as its collection of paintings by the Bassano family, the museum possesses a number of paintings by other Venetian artists, including some good works by Tiepolo, as well as ceramics, for which the town is famous, and designs by Canova, the neoclassical sculptor who was born nearby at Possagno in 1757. Canova is best known for his classical reliefs and cold, highly finished statues, often tinged with a hint of eroticism, as in the famous statue of Pauline Borghese in the Villa Borghese in Rome. He is not seen as a typical Venetian artist, probably because our image of eighteenth-century Venice is one of unbridled decadence, the world of Casanova, Goldoni and Vivaldi, where English aristocrats on the Grand Tour could indulge their every whim, sexual or otherwise, during Carnival, and return home laden with the works of Canaletto.

Antonio Canova, the leading neoclassical sculptor, numbered among his patrons kings, princes and emperors. Works from all periods of his career can be found in his home town of Possagno.

In fact, Antonio Canova (1757-1822) became the leading Italian neoclassical artist, the favourite sculptor of royalty and nobility all over the continent. To gain a full understanding of the range of his sculpture, take the Montebelluna road for 5km east of Bassano, and, turning left, follow the signs through Crespano del Grappa to Possagno. The road winds through low, conical hills, covered in vines which produce some excellent white wine.

In true neoclassical style, the village of Possagno is dominated by the dome of the Temple of Canova (1819-30), modelled on the Pantheon. Further down the hill stands the Gipsoteca, which houses a comprehensive collection of Canova's statues, models and reliefs. They greatly enhance the sculptor's reputation, which has suffered under the demise of neo-

Opposite: The picturesque town of Bassano del Grappa with its covered Ponte degli Alpini seen against the backdrop of the Dolomites.
Right: A statue of Ceres rises before the walls of Castelfranco.

classicism. There is much to admire: the lively early reliefs of the Labours of Hercules, the charming dog watching Endymion sleeping, the vast and powerful bust of the Rezzonico Pope Clement XIV (a great patron of Canova's Venetian contemporary Piranesi), and the bronze horse modelled on those which, until their recent disgraceful removal, adorned the façade of St Mark's in Venice.

Many of Canova's religious commissions are derivative, some of his reliefs uninspiring, and his nudes rather off-putting, with their frigid eroticism and precariously placed fig leaves, but the overall quality of the carving is very high. This is particularly true of the vibrant spontaniety of his *bozzetti* (sketches). Certainly, the model of Titian's tomb is much superior to the feeble monument in the Frari in Venice, and the model for the Three Graces seems much finer than the finished version recently sold by the Duke of Bedford (known dismissively in the art world as the Three Bottoms). Upstairs, there is a good portrait of Sir Thomas Lawrence by Canova and a pathetic statue of the tragic King of Rome (Napoleon's son) as Cupid, showing Canova's cosmopolitan connections.

STRONGHOLDS OF THE SERENISSIMA

SOAVE · MAROSTICA · MONTAGNANA

The fortified town of Soave stands on a hillside in a wonderful position overlooking vineyards which stretch to the horizon.

Most of us are still strongly influenced by the Victorians' love of the Middle Ages, with its stirring tales of chivalry, its knights errant in their gleaming armour setting out to rescue damsels imprisoned in impenetrable castles. Nowhere is this atmosphere better evoked than in the fortified towns of the Veneto. The piazza in Marostica, where two love-stricken rivals played chess for the fair hand of the Venetian Governor's daughter; the keep of Soave, with its heraldic emblems, and the ramparts of Montagnana perfectly capture this bygone age.

The Veneto, like so much of Italy, had a violent history all through the Middle Ages, as the small city-states fought for supremacy and independence. These struggles were part of a larger conflict between supporters of popes and emperors, known as Guelphs and Ghibellines respectively. The warrior kings of the north came seeking money from the Italian banks, often, as in the case of Edward III in 1339, bankrupting their unfortunate creditors when they defaulted on their loans; crusaders embarked from the ports; and there was seldom a year when some new invading force did not appear over the Alps, eager to sample the rich pickings of the south.

In this violent age, it is scarcely surprising that Italy should have been at the forefront of military technology. This was the supreme age of castle building, before the introduction of gunpowder. The Normans in the south, followed by the Emperor Frederick II, were master engineers, erecting massive donjons and curtain walls to protect strategic points in their kingdoms. The defenders of these castles were virtually invincible except by starvation, disease or treachery. The city-states of the Veneto, however, did not possess such resources, and their forts, built on a more modest scale, were taken and

retaken as the wars ebbed and flowed across northern Italy. This chaos was only brought to an end when the various city-states came under the domination of Venice in the fourteenth and fifteenth centuries.

One surprising relic of these bloodthirsty times is the number of fortified towns which have survived with their walls intact. This itinerary takes in three of the most complete of these. Soave, like Marostica, has the advantage of a superb natural position, with lines of fortification crowning the hillside. The town, best known for its white wine, which has, unfortunately, earned an unenviable reputation for its mediocre quality due to ludicrous over-commercialization, lies midway between Verona and Vicenza, just north of the main A4 *autostrada*.

The Scaligers, the most remarkable of Verona's rulers, greatly enlarged and strengthened the fort in the fourteenth century, and the battlements have the characteristic Ghibelline swallowtail crenellations. Verona was a stout champion of the Empire against the Papacy, and one of the first places that Dante came to after he was exiled from Guelph Florence. In theory, you can always tell a town's allegiance from the shape of its crenellations. In practice, the Ghibelline swallowtail motif is so much more picturesque than the more prosaic Guelph square battlements that the Guelphs often adopted it, so you need to beware before showing off your knowledge of Italian medieval history. This is particularly true where there has been nineteenth-century restoration.

Soave is enclosed in a complete set of walls, running up to the keep at the summit of the hill. On such a precipitous site, it was difficult to build a large fort. The Scaligers concentrated, therefore, on raising the height of the walls, and increasing their thickness, to protect the defenders from missiles. The tower of the

Starting-point: Soave
Recommended time: Full day
Length of tour: 80 miles (130km)
Best time of year: May/June or September/October
Finishing-point: Montagnana

keep has been largely restored, the rooms decorated in a style reminiscent of William Morris with animals and the Scala motif of a ladder (a pun on *scala*, the Italian for ladder, or staircase). On the outer staircase a dog holds a coat of arms with the Scala motif, probably a reference to the eccentric nicknames for the Scaliger rulers: Cangrande (Big Dog), Cansignorio (Lord Dog) and Mastino (Mastiff). Above, a series of warriors' heads wearing helmets are fixed to the balustrade, some with visors open, some shut. After the demise of the Scaligers, Soave passed to the Visconti of Milan then to Venice in 1405.

The view from the keep is very impressive, particularly to the north, where the vines, which grow right up to the castle walls, stretch across the hills into the distance. From this height the town below looks almost deserted, with just the occasional figure emerging from the solitary bar in the main street.

Marostica is in an even better state of preservation than Soave. It lies on the far side of Vicenza, some 28km north on the road to Bassano. The setting is very dramatic, with the hills pressing right up behind the battlements. The town occupies a key strategic position, and was taken many times, by the Paduan tyrant Ezzelino da Romano, one of the most bloodthirsty of all medieval rulers, in 1236, and subsequently by Vicenza, Padua and Verona, whose rulers built most of the fortifications. Like Soave, it fell to Venice in 1405, but was briefly recaptured once more, by the Emperor Maximilian in 1509.

The most famous feature of the town, visible as soon as you enter the main gate, is the piazza laid out in the form of a chessboard. This commemorates a legendary chess match in 1554 between Rinaldo d'Angorano and Vieri da Vallonara for the hand of Lionara, the daughter of the Venetian Governor Taddeo Parisio. Chess players are not noted for their good manners, but this match was played in a spirit of chivalry with a happy ending, one contestant win-

ning Lionara and the other her sister Oldrada. Every alternate September the match is replayed, with commentary in archaic Venetian dialect, totally unintelligible to you and me, and to spectators and participants alike. This induces a general element of farce and produces moves which would confuse even the most experienced grand master.

Above the piazza two wings of fortifications rise to the fort on top of the hill, built by Cangrande della Scala in the fourteenth century. For the energetic, the Strada Panoramica zigzags up the hill between cypresses, olives, figs and the ubiquitous vines. The walls of the fort are built in a picturesque mixture of red brick and white stone. From the summit there is a superb view across the plain, interrupted by a series of campanili rising up like sentinels.

The third of the fortified towns is an unlikely survival from the Middle Ages. Montagnana lies in the flat country that stretches south of Padua and Vicenza towards the Po valley.

From Marostica head south to the A31. Turn off at Vicenza Est and continue south on the SS247. After 35km turn right on to the SS10 for Montagnana.

Without the natural advantages of a hilly site, the town changed hands endlessly, including a mind-boggling thirteen times during the War of the League of Cambrai between Venice and the Empire at the beginning of the sixteenth century. Nevertheless, it possesses a number of fine buildings, including Palladio's Villa Pisani beside the Porta Padova, the red brick Duomo, with its elegant Renaissance portal, by Lorenzo Bregno, and a luminous Veronese 'Transfiguration' over the high altar, and numerous fine palaces around the central Piazza Vittorio Emanuele.

The walls themselves, stretching for over a mile in circumference, were built by Ezzelino da Romano between 1242 and 1259 and elaborated by Francesco da Schicci a century later. The web of fortifications surrounding the gates, one for each axis, the twenty-four pentagonal towers, and the stoutly defended bridge outside the Porta Legnago, are almost

The picturesque piazza of Marostica, beneath the lines of fortification, is laid out in the shape of a chessboard. Every other September a match is played, using real people as pieces.

The perfectly preserved walls and towers of Montagnana date back to the Middle Ages. A jousting ground beside the moat is still used for tournaments.

Opposite: The intricate battlements of the Scaliger fortifications crown the town of Soave. Right: The jousting ground in front of the Porta Legnago at Montagnana, the best preserved of all fortified towns in the Veneto.

perfectly preserved. Their high walls, topped by elaborate machicolations, designed for pouring burning oil on the besiegers, and strengthened by numerous towers, are typical of the period. The height of the walls enabled the defenders to rain missiles on the siege towers, battering-rams and scaling ladders brought up by the attacking army. They also provided defence from the projectiles and ballistae hurled from catapults. Once armies began to use cannon in the fifteenth century, these fortifications proved inadequate, and were soon breached.

Montagnana, like Soave and Marostica, belongs to the world of the late Middle Ages – a world of battles, chivalry and courtly love. The best way to experience this medieval atmosphere is to attend the annual jousting tournament on the open ground beyond the moat, preferably after a meal in the excellent Aldo Moro restaurant. It is easy to imagine the authentic knights in full armour, with their pennants flying, entering the lists, the ladies in their taffeta dresses and velvet gowns, and the crowd cheering on its champions.

TOUR 11

ILLUSIONS OF GRANDEUR

VILLA CORDELLINA · VILLA VALMARANA · VILLA PISANI, STRA

The Palladian-style Villa Cordellina has two notable paintings by Tiepolo which hang in the central hall.

The Republic of Venice, which played such an illustrious role on the pages of European history, lasted a thousand years. At her zenith she controlled, in her own proud words, 'a quarter, and half a quarter', of the ancient Roman Empire. By the eighteenth century, all that remained was the splendour of her own image, on which all Europe flocked to gaze. Like a setting sun, the rays of her artistic genius continued to illuminate Italian painting, and her leading artists were fêted from Madrid to St Petersburg. Canaletto's views were the pride and joy of many a Grand Tourist's collection, Longhi's masked figures evoke the excitement of life in her salons and boudoirs, and Guardi's atmospheric capriccios prefigure the romantic passion for Venice.

But the artist who best captures this glorious Venetian swansong is Giambattista Tiepolo (1696-1770), the favourite of kings and princes throughout Europe. Tiepolo shares the predilections of all the greatest Venetian painters. Highly imaginative and prolific, revelling in the sensuous effects of light and colour, he was equally at home dashing off vast acres of fresco or sketching the most intimate drawing in red chalk. Such is the fickleness of taste, however, that almost immediately after his death, his work was dismissed as superficial, and within a generation, with the demise of the Serenissima at the hands of Napoleon, Venice and her most famous eighteenth-century artist drifted into obscurity together.

The Veneto possesses three of his finest works, all easily visited within a day: the Villa Valmarana, decorated on a very human scale by him and his son Gian Domenico, the Villa Cordellina, with two of his most powerful classical works, and the Villa Pisani at Stra, the ultimate in ostentatious splendour.

The Villa Cordellina, at Montecchio Maggiore,

lies some 10km west of Vicenza off the SS11 just after Tavernelle; if you are on the A4 *autostrada* between Vicenza and Verona, take the Montecchio exit. The villa, built by Giorgio Massari between 1735 and 1760, is a handsome building in the Palladian style. It shows the enormous influence Palladio still exerted in his home province almost two centuries after his death, and exactly coincides with the Palladian movement that was sweeping England at the time. The garden, with its impressive gate piers, its numerous statues grouped around the fountain, and its central focus on the house, is a typical baroque design.

Inside the villa, the central hall is dominated by two large paintings by Giambattista Tiepolo, the 'Family of Darius before Alexander' and the 'Continence of Scipio'. Executed for the lawyer Carlo Cordellina in 1743-4, they depict two of the greatest generals of antiquity sitting in judgement over their defeated enemies. Eminently suitable subjects for a man of the law, both Alexander and Scipio display their compassion and wisdom in sparing the vanquished. The splendour of the scenes, and the grandeur of the High Renaissance architecture, hark back to the paintings of Veronese, during the golden age of Venetian painting.

Tiepolo's instinctive sympathies seem to lie with the women, the wife and aging mother on their knees before Alexander, begging for mercy, and the proud girl advancing towards Scipio. These women are portrayed in sumptuous costumes, which shimmer as the light catches the silken folds of their draperies. The two generals, on the other hand, seem to merge with their backgrounds, so that it is difficult to form any impression of their characters. On the ceiling above, Fame trumpets the union of Glory and Virtue.

Starting-point: Villa Cordellina

Recommended time: Full day

Length of tour: 37 miles (60km)

Best time of year: May/June or September/October

Finishing-point: Villa Pisani, Stra

The Villa Valmarana is one of the most charming villas in the Veneto, with delightful frescoes by Giambattista Tiepolo and his son Gian Domenico.

As you approach Vicenza, you will see the Villa Valmarana on the slope of Monte Berico overlooking the town. To reach it, turn right just after passing the railway station. Like the Villa Cordellina, it is yet another example of the Palladian style, by Francesco Muttoni, and dates from 1668, with four symmetrical rooms grouped around a central hall. The garden wall flanking the villa is surmounted by a series of grotesque statues of dwarves, the ancestors of all garden gnomes. The story goes that once upon a time the owner had a daughter who was a dwarf. In order to hide her deformity, he surrounded her with fellow dwarves. For many years she dwelt in blissful ignorance until, one fateful day, looking out of the window, she saw a tall, handsome youth and, realizing the terrible truth, flung herself to her death. Hence the villa's true name, the Villa Valmarana dei Nani. How little does the garden gnome suspect his tragic origins!

The frescoes in the villa, painted for Count Giustino Valmarana in 1757, have serious, moral themes, but are much more decorative than those in the Villa Cordellina. They are given a lighter-hearted note by the *trompe-l'oeil* architectural frames painted round the scenes by Mengozzi Colonna. Giambattista takes episodes from Homer, Euripides, Virgil, Tasso and Ariosto, and concentrates on the themes of love and devotion to duty. The heroes, in dastardly fashion, enjoy the former to the full, before plumping for the latter, leaving their lovestruck women bewailing their fate. Aeneas abandons the luckless Dido, just as Rinaldo is torn from the arms of Armida. Achilles, mourning for Briseis by the seashore, in one of Tiepolo's most poignant images, is persuaded by his mother Thetis to vent his fury on the Trojans rather than the Greek king Agamemnon.

In the hall Agamemnon himself, his face buried in his cloak, consents to the sacrifice of his daughter Iphigenia so that the Greek fleet can set sail for Troy. Our eyes are drawn upwards from the central group of Iphigenia and the priest by the altar, to the goddess Diana, who dispatches a deer on a cloud to replace her. In the centre of the ceiling two putti blow for all their worth, and a gust of wind stirs the sails of the becalmed Greek fleet.

In these frescoes Tiepolo displays his gifts to the full. The emotions of the participants are conveyed by their gestures; passion alternates with anguish and despair. Colonna's fictive framework, within which the figures move, varies from the rococo curves of the scenes from Tasso and Ariosto to the sterner classical backdrop of the episodes from the *Iliad*.

The Foresteria, or garden house, by the main gate, contains more frescoes by the Tiepolos, almost entirely by the son Gian Domenico. While his father was recreating the world of the classics, he filled the rooms of this small building with delightful scenes of country life. The peasants picnicking beneath the trees, and the lovers walking through the landscape, are frequently cited as the precursors of the realistic painters of the nineteenth century. But the operatic quality of their idyllic lifestyle is closer to the world of Gainsborough's fancy paintings, and to Marie Antoinette and her maids dressed as shepherdesses, than the darker world of Goya, whom Giambattista and Gian Domenico probably met when they departed for Spain in 1762.

In the Chinese room Gian Domenico has imagined the world of the Orient, with altars to pagan gods, exotic birds and merchants displaying marvellous silks for sale. The last room on the left, not always open to the public, conjures up the hedonistic world of the Venetian Carnival. Every room looks out on to the green Valle del Silenzio, one of the most beautiful landscapes in the Veneto.

Before leaving Vicenza, do not miss Palladio's Villa Rotonda, which stands just to the east of the Villa Valmarana. Follow the path running downhill, turn right at the bottom and the Rotonda is about 100 metres up the road. The most famous of all Palladio's villas, a pleasure pavilion on a hilltop with four porticoes gazing out over the surrounding landscape, the Villa Rotonda proved immensely influential on Georgian architecture in England and America.

Top: Gian Domenico
Tiepolo's delightful fresco
of young lovers in a winter
landscape, and (bottom)
of an old woman gathering
eggs, are both to be found in
the Foresteria of the Villa
Valmarana outside Vicenza.
Opposite: The grandiose
façade of the Villa Pisani at
Stra overlooks the Brenta
canal.

The third villa on this itinerary is the Villa Pisani at Stra, on the banks of the Brenta canal. Take the A1 *autostrada* towards Padua and Venice, and turn off at the Padova Est exit. Stra is the first village on the road running east of the city.

The Villa Pisani is a gigantic structure overlooking the Brenta. The long façade, the central section designed like a temple front supported by caryatids, is the grandest in the Veneto. It is the Venetian equivalent of Versailles, an extravagant baroque adaptation of Palladio. The villa demonstrates the pompous pretensions of the Pisani family, which reached their apogee when Alvise Pisani was elected Doge of Venice in 1735. He had already commissioned Frigimelica to design a villa for his country seat, but he now called in Francesco Maria Preti to increase the splendour of the building dramatically.

The villa has always appealed to those with delusions of grandeur. Russian and Austrian emperors, kings, dictators and megalomaniacs flocked to visit it. Napoleon was so impressed by it during his stay in 1807 that he gave the villa to his stepson Eugène de Beauharnais, and Mussolini chose the villa for his first meeting with Hitler in 1934.

The vast interior, built around two courtyards, has been virtually denuded of its original furnishings and, apart from some eighteenth-century landscapes and mythological scenes by Zuccarelli and Guarana, there is nothing to delay you passing through to the ballroom, with its magnificent ceiling by Tiepolo. This, the 'Apotheosis of the House of Pisani', painted in 1761-2, shortly before the Tiepolo family departed for Spain, represents the ultimate in social climbing. Fame trumpets the glory of the Pisani family, who are grouped among allegorical figures of the Arts and Virtues. The Pisani heir, in his blue suit, is seated securely in the lap of Venice. Around the perimeter, Evil and Heresy are put to flight. In one corner, perhaps to relieve the pomposity of the whole scene, a drunken man's leg protrudes beneath a table.

The 'Apotheosis of the House of Pisani' is a triumph of illusionism as Tiepolo effortlessly creates the impression of his figures floating far up in the sky. The warm colours, pinks, golds and yellows, increase in intensity towards the centre. Studiously ignoring the advent of neoclassicism, with its demands for accuracy and realism, Tiepolo seems to have been content to perfect a make-believe world of pleasure and beauty. To the high-minded this may smack of superficiality, but to all those who love art for its own sake, Tiepolo's absolute mastery of composition, his brilliant colours and his fluid brushwork, make him one of the most attractive of all eighteenth-century painters.

The park, landscaped in the French style, is equally magnificent, filled with classical pavilions and gazebos half-hidden among the lime trees. The central canal, flanked by statues of classical gods, leads from the villa to Frigimelica's palatial stable block, with a series of statues crowning the façade. This vista, and the scale of the stables, increases the illusion of the size of the park. An intricate maze to the right allowed the Doge and his friends full scope for clandestine liaisons. Sailing up the Brenta canal in his stately barge, away from the stifling heat of the city, Pisani must have felt that he was arriving in paradise.

IMPERIAL INHERITANCE

AQUILEIA · GRADO · CIVIDALE

The Basilica of Aquileia, with its magnificent mosaic floor, is one of the most impressive churches in Italy. The town has extensive remains from the ancient Roman port on the site.

Late antiquity was a turbulent time, as rival pretenders fought for the imperial crown, and hordes of Vandals and Goths gathered on the borders of the Roman Empire. Despite the splendour of its civic architecture, the confidence engendered by the Pax Romana, which had held good for centuries, seemed to be disappearing. Men questioned the ancient gods and sought solace in the new religions which arose in the East. The most popular and enduring of these, despite prolonged periods of persecution, was Christianity, a creed which drew followers from all classes and walks of life.

With the advent of Constantine, the first Christian Emperor, at the beginning of the fourth century, Christians were able to worship openly. They erected churches all over the Empire, many of them on the burial sites of martyrs. Artistic forms were given a new inspiration, in particular the basilican shape of classical temples, which was now used for churches. One of the finest examples is the Basilica in Aquileia, a miraculous survival of centuries of conflict. You need to devote a whole morning to the large site of Aquileia, leaving the afternoon for the early Christian churches of Grado, or the exquisite Tempietto Longobardo at Cividale.

Like the better known Torcello and Ravenna further down the Adriatic coast, the town of Aquileia, tucked away in the north-east corner of Italy, but within easy reach of Venice, maintained strong links with Constantinople during the dying days of the Roman Empire. The town was founded in 181BC, and soon became the capital of a large and strategically important province encompassing Friuli, the Veneto and parts of north-western Yugoslavia. Enough remains of the ancient Forum, harbour, markets and warehouses, to enable you to visualize its days of glory. Augustus settled a new colony here, used Aquileia as his headquarters during campaigns against the barbarians, and chose the site for his meeting with Herod the Great in 10BC. Two centuries later, the Emperor Constantius resided in a splendid palace here for many years before dying in Aquileia in AD340.

The town survived Attila the Hun's sack in AD452, and continued to flourish artistically while all around collapsed into chaos. Gradually, the harbour silted up with sand, the surrounding marshes became infected with malaria, and the locals used the ruins as a quarry. But Aquileia's fame endured, and, right down to the Renaissance, the Patriarchate of Aquileia was one of the most important posts in the Catholic church.

You might begin by making a swift visit to the Archaeological Museum. The collection consists of a wide variety of statues, including some good portrait busts, cameos, intaglios, a fine bronze chandelier, endless inscriptions and mosaics depicting an extraordinary variety of fish. Less comprehensive, but more digestible to the layman, is the Paleo-Christian Museum at the north-eastern corner of the site. It is housed in an open hall resembling a basilica, the ground floor covered in mosaics. A raised wooden platform takes you down the length of the hall, giving an excellent view of the bright blue and red geometric patterns of the mosaics, many of them washed by a green slime as though they had just been rescued from the bed of the sea. Upstairs, there are more mosaics of animals and Christian reliefs depicting Christ, Lazarus and a baptism.

Leaving the museum, you can enjoy the most atmospheric approach to the patriarchal Basilica. Entering by the Porto Fluviale Romano (and

Starting-point: Aquileia
Recommended time: Very full day or a day and a half
Length of tour: 42 miles (68km)
Best time of year: May/June or September/October
Finishing-point: Cividale

Opposite: The majestic interior of the patriarchal Basilica at Aquileia features free-standing Corinthian columns and a remarkable mosaic floor.

Left: A charming, naïve fresco of the Adoration of the Magi, surrounded by crisp, naturalistic carving, painted on the ceiling of the Tempietto Longobardo at Cividale.

ignoring, in true Italian fashion, a sign marked *Uscita* – meaning exit), you walk down an avenue of cypresses, with the old walls of the harbour on your right, and a row of umbrella pines beyond. Once these wharves and jetties, built of white Istrian stone to prevent salt-water corrosion, teemed with sailors, fishermen, merchants and workmen, rigging and fitting out their ships, unloading their catch, haggling over the price of their wares, and drinking and carousing in the taverns.

This approach also offers the best view of the Basilica, set within a grove of cypresses and guarded by a massive fortified campanile, built in the eleventh century with stone taken from the amphitheatre. If you are unlucky enough to encounter busloads of tourists, you can beat a hasty retreat and investigate other parts of the town. The best time to visit the church is either first thing in the morning, or during the lunch hour, when everyone else has departed.

The Basilica, dedicated to the Virgin and saints Hermagora and Fortunatus (obscure, even by early Christian standards), was begun in 313. What we see today, however, is very much later, and offers a fascinating juxtaposition of styles. The exterior, like the campanile, is plain Romanesque with a minimum of decoration. The interior, on the other hand, is very much earlier, with a Paleo-Christian mosaic floor and classical Corinthian columns marching up the nave, surmounted by Gothic rows of arches and a medieval wooden ship's keel ceiling. Because of the simplicity of the architecture, and the magnificent quality of all the details, this combination works extremely well.

Miraculously, the vast mosaic floor, originally commissioned by Bishop Theodore shortly after building was begun, was covered over in the Middle Ages, and has therefore remained almost perfectly preserved. It demonstrates the extraordinary sophistication of mosaicists working in late antiquity, and compares with contemporary paving at Piazza Armerina (see page 135). The later medieval floor was only removed in 1909-12. The charm of the mosaics lies in their spontaneity and the richness of their colours.

The mosaicists display, at every opportunity, their love of the natural world.

They are also filled with complex Christian iconography. The fight between the cock and turtle, on the right by the door, represents the struggle between Christ (like the cock the bringer of light) and the devil (like the turtle dwelling in darkness). A bag of money is placed between the contestants and, further up the nave, the victorious cock is awarded an olive branch and a laurel crown, and bread and grapes, symbolizing the Eucharist.

The most interesting section of the floor, in front of the altar steps, depicts the story of Jonah. As befits the inhabitants of a port, the mosaicists were inspired in their portrayal of every form of aquatic life, from octopuses and sea monsters to ducks, as they are pursued by fishermen (probably a reference to Christ's wish to make his disciples 'fishers of men'). At the centre of the composition Jonah is swallowed by a serpent-like whale, despite the best efforts of a sailor to clutch on to his legs, and then vomited up after three days, symbolizing Christ's death and resurrection. The most amusing scene is on the right, where Jonah relaxes beneath a pumpkin bower – a vivid impression of the artist's idea of paradise.

In the right aisle, in another example of the mosaicists' love of nature, Christ is set among a veritable menagerie, with stags and antelopes grazing peacefully next to partridges. The exceptional durability of these mosaics compares favourably with the damaged twelfth-century frescoes of the life of St Hermagora in the crypt beneath the apse. The sculptors in the Basilica rival the mosaicists in their depictions of animals and birds, both in the carved screens off the right apse, and the angels and paschal lamb carved on the red marble sarcophagus adjoining it.

In the Cripta degli Scavi on the left of the Basilica more mosaics have been uncovered, including another battle royal between a cock and a turtle, an excellent leaping donkey, and a delectable lobster. To my mind this Basilica, in the quality of its works of art, and the strength of its atmosphere, captures the world of late antiquity every bit as well as the more famous churches of Ravenna.

Before leaving the town, do not miss the small cemetery (follow the yellow signs to the Sepolcretto). Set outside the town walls, as required by Roman law, the five plots, with their sarcophagi and votive altars, are filled with images of the next world: pomegranates, quinces, dolphins (symbolizing the final journey across the ocean), and winged guardian spirits with lowered torches. Squashed between the present villagers' plots, with vines on one side, and beds of irises and spring onions on the other, and cypresses towering above, this burial ground is perhaps the most evocative part of Aquileia.

Grado possesses plenty of early Christian mosaics in a similar style to those at Aquileia.

Beyond Aquileia, in an island on the edge of the lagoon, lies the fishing town of Grado. The Duomo, as at Aquileia dedicated to saints Hermagora and Fortunatus (obviously local bigwigs), has a similar fortified appearance on the exterior, with a bulky, square campanile acting as a look-out post. The interior follows the basilican plan, with a fine sixth-century mosaic floor. The design is more stylized than that of the Basilica at Aquileia, with the names of the donors inscribed in geometrical borders over the whole area of the floor.

The locals treated the vast classical legacy that lay all around them in the most cavalier fashion. A random selection of columns adorns the nave, all taken piecemeal from Roman buildings, and crowned with a variety of Byzantine capitals. The curious ambo, or pulpit, is equally eclectic, with classical and medieval components, including Venetian Gothic arches. Adjoining the Duomo is the octagonal Baptistery, and across the Campo dei Patriarchi lies the simple church of Santa Maria delle Grazie, possibly dating from the fifth century, with fine mosaics and a marble screen featuring peacocks.

The exquisite carving of the tiny Tempietto Longobardo at Cividale is a very rare survival of the Dark Ages.

A further precious survival of the Dark Ages lies hidden in the centre of the province of Friuli. From Grado return to Aquileia and head north-

east towards Gorizia before taking the SS305, followed by the 356, to Cividale. The vines covering these rolling hills produce delicious fruity white wine, in my view the best in Italy. The ancient town of Cividale overlooks the steep banks of the River Natisone. Originally named Forum Iuli in honour of Julius Caesar, from which the name Friuli derives, it was the chief seat of the Patriarchs of Aquileia from the eighth to the thirteenth century, and the capital of Berengar I, King of all Italy from 888 to 924. There are two major artistic sites in Cividale: the famous Tempietto Longobardo and the Museo Cristiano in the Duomo. The museum houses the simple, elegant Baptismal Font of Patriarch Callixtus as well as the Altar of Ratchis, Duke of Friuli, a masterpiece of eighth-century Lombardic sculpture depicting Christ in Majesty, the Visitation and Adoration of the Magi.

The Tempietto Longobardo stands in a picturesque position overlooking the river, a five-minute walk from the bridge (follow the signs). It is the only surviving part of an eighth-century Lombard church. For those seeking atmosphere, and who desire to escape the crowds who have ruined so many of the most famous sites in Italy, this intimate little room possesses it in abundance. The beauty of the marble columns, and the crispness of the carving, both of the capitals and of the vines and leaves on the arch over the altar, are of the highest quality. On either side of the arch stand martyred saints, holding their crowns above their heads. On the ceiling of the dome is a charming and naïve fresco of the Adoration of the Magi, and the figure of Christ in a *mandorla*. These works of art, in Cividale, Aquileia and Grado, precious survivals of the Dark Ages and well worth visiting, show the vital role this area of Italy played in preserving the classical legacy for its triumphant rediscovery in the Renaissance.

UMBRIA AND
THE MARCHE

T he provinces of Umbria and the Marche, with their panoramic landscapes, are clustered below the peaks of the Apennines, the backbone of Italy. Turning inland from the Adriatic coastline, or leaving the upper Tiber valley, you enter the true rural Italy. The beauty of the countryside has scarcely altered since the time of St Francis, Umbria's most popular saint – wind rustles over a field of ripening corn, clouds scud over an upland meadow, carpeted with wild flowers, pigs dig for the highly prized truffles beneath an ancient oak tree, and the resin of pine needles fills the air. Old men play bowls in the sand beneath the walls of Urbino as their fathers and grandfathers did before them, and you can enjoy a delicious meal of game cooked on a grill and spit over wood embers, the staple implements of local cooking since time immemorial.

Both Umbria and the Marche enjoyed a period of prosperity and independence in the early Middle Ages. Each town proclaimed its superiority over its neighbours by erecting magnificent palaces and churches. The defensive siting of Umbria's towns on precipitous hilltops allowed her architects full scope for their sense of drama. Invariably, the Duomo and the most important *palazzi* dominate the view, and are approached by a steep flight of steps. Even if one's only knowledge of the province is a glimpse from the *autostrada* while hurrying from Florence to Rome, the stepped façade of the Duomo of Orvieto, set against the sky, makes an unforgettable impact.

The competitive nature of the Umbrian towns led to endless feuds throughout the Middle Ages. Indeed, so warlike were the Baglioni, the rulers of Perugia, that their children were said to be born with a sword in their hands. It was to combat this natural aggression that St Francis of Assisi, who had himself been a soldier in his youth, began preaching in the towns and villages of his native countryside. The most attractive of Italy's myriad saints, so many of whom came from Umbria, St Francis was a passionate lover of beauty and the natural world. Something of his gentleness still imbues the landscape, and the chief characteristics of the Umbrian school of painting, which reached its heyday in the fifteenth century, are a sweetness of expression in the hundreds of representations of the Madonna and Child, and a softness in the depiction of the landscape, where the background dissolves into a colour known as Umbrian blue.

By this time the Papacy controlled most of the province. Cardinal Albornoz, a brilliant general who had led the King of Spain's armies to victory over the Moors, reconquered the Marche and part of Umbria in the mid-fourteenth century, and his successors gradually subdued the remaining warring towns over the next two centuries. With the loss of their independence, their magnificent civic buildings fell into disuse, their most ambitious and talented sons left to pursue their fortunes in Rome, and the towns became backwaters. This accounts for the astonishing survival of their medieval architecture.

There are a number of attractive bases from which to visit Umbria, and you can take your pick between Perugia, the provincial capital, Assisi and Spoleto. A stay in Perugia allows you to explore the wealth of Peruginos in the galleries and churches, the exquisite sculpture of Agostino di Duccio on the façade of the Oratory of San Bernardino, and the extraordinary escalator dug through the ruins of the ancient city so that you appear to be descending through a Piranesi etching. Assisi, spread across the slopes of Mount Subasio, is a better preserved medieval town than Perugia, and, by staying there, you can enjoy its charm in the evening after the hordes of tourists and pilgrims have departed. Spoleto, with its Roman ruins and Romanesque churches, is, possibly, the most picturesque of the three, but if you are unlucky enough to coincide with the Festival of the Two Worlds, you will find it flooded with beautiful people sipping their fill from the well of culture.

The Marche's charms are harder to uncover because of their relative inaccessibility. The road network is designed like a comb, so that you are constantly being drawn back to the motorway linking the horrors of the Adriatic coast. Fortunately, Urbino and Ascoli Piceno lie sufficiently far inland to have been spared, and remain two of the most fascinating towns in central Italy. Certainly, the achievements of Federico da Montefeltro in Urbino and the glittering array of artists he attracted to his ducal court, have endured through the centuries.

Urbino is the obvious place to stay in the Marche, but the province is very spread out and, if you enjoy the challenge of discovering remote altar-pieces by Lorenzo Lotto or Carlo Crivelli, two Renaissance artists who escaped from the pressures of life in cosmopolitan Venice to work in this remote region, you will need to drive long distances. Many of Lotto's most important works are now housed in the museums of Iesi and Recanati, but Crivelli's altar-pieces, with the exception of his masterpiece in the Duomo of Ascoli Piceno, still hang in little village churches tucked away in the hills.

You can spend a fascinating day searching them out. Crivelli, imprisoned in Venice in 1457 for hiding away the wife of an absent sailor, and for 'knowing her carnally in contempt of God and of Holy Matrimony', retreated to the Marche in search of anonymity. He found it in the little villages of Massa Fermana, Monte San Martino and Montefiore dell' Aso. Each village lies off the SS210, which runs from Macerata to Amandola. The road has superb views over the Monti Sibillini, one of the highest ranges of the Apennines. No one will disturb your enjoyment of these beautiful altar-pieces, with their powerful figures breaking free from their archaic Gothic frames and gold backgrounds. You are in good company here. The priest of the church in Monte San Martino will hasten to point out Prince Charles's signature in the visitors' book.

The towns of the Marche are full of interest – and much of the countryside is very beautiful – but, with the exception of Urbino, they do not rival Umbria in the quality of their works of art. My favourite view in Umbria is across the valley from the ancient Etruscan city of Perugia. On a fine evening, go down to the church of San Pietro, which stands at its southern limit, beyond the walls. Ask the sacristan if you can see the view (*belvedere* in Italian), and he will lead you behind the high altar, and open the double doors, covered in fine intarsia work. A little balcony stands high above the road. The landscape opens out beneath your feet, a patchwork of olive groves, vineyards, and fields of corn and maize. In the middle distance the sun picks out the white buildings of Assisi, nestled in the lee of Mount Subasio. Beyond, the valley winds on to Foligno and Spoleto. The whole history of Umbria lies at your feet.

TOUR 13

PERUGINO'S MASTERPIECES

CITTA DELLA PIEVE · PANICALE · CONVENT OF SANT' AGNESE, PERUGIA

The town of Città della Pieve possesses one masterpiece by Perugino, its famous native son. His 'Adoration of the Magi' is one of the most beautiful paintings in Umbria.

Starting-point: Città della Pieve

Recommended time: Short day

Length of tour: 40 miles (65km)

Best time of year: April/June or September/October

Finishing-point: Perugia

Perugino (c.1445-1523) encapsulates the charm and complexity of Umbria. A painter famed for his exquisite depictions of the Madonna and Child, some of the most perfect creations of the Quattrocento, Perugino was himself a confirmed atheist. This strange dichotomy between his character and his art is echoed in Umbria's medieval history, where the enormous popularity of St Francis, who spent almost his entire career in his home province, had little effect upon the savagery of the internecine feuds between the various city states. This curious contrast between barbarism and religion characterizes the opening chapter of the Renaissance.

As the most famous of all Umbrian painters, Perugino's output was very prolific and often of uneven quality. This was partly because he left many commissions to his pupils, and partly because he was too often content to repeat a well-worn, if successful and lucrative, formula. To experience the full range of his genius, it is essential to go to Umbria and see his paintings in their original settings. Only then can you understand why, in Vasari's words, his contemporaries 'rushed like madmen' to look at them when they first appeared.

You will also be able to study the mind of the artist and to appreciate the problems that he had to surmount. A religious work of art always loses some of its impact when transferred to a secular building. There is also the profound satisfaction in discovering something for oneself, leaving behind the coach parties and organized tours. You may have to pay for it; the sacristan may be taking his siesta and not to be disturbed, or the painting may be '*in restauro*', but that merely adds a *frisson* of excitement to the expedition.

Now that Piero della Francesca has been 'discovered', Perugino is, perhaps, the best artist to study

in this way. By chance several of his greatest paintings are still in Umbria and can be seen in their original settings. Furthermore, Panicale and Città della Pieve have barely changed since the Renaissance, and the surrounding countryside, the soft, rolling hills covered in feathery cypresses, with distant views over the still waters of Lake Trasimene, comes straight from the background of a Perugino fresco.

The mellow red brick town of Città della Pieve, the birthplace of Perugino, possesses an outstanding altar-piece by the master. After a quick look inside the Duomo, memorable as much for its eccentric sacristan, reputedly the illegitimate son of a local priest, as for a bland Baptism by Perugino, head down Via dei Bianchi to the chapel of Santa Maria dei Bianchi. The instructions on the door for finding the sacristan (a man after the artist's own heart and not averse to a decent tip), are, for once, surprisingly reliable.

The altar-piece of the Adoration of the Magi, covering the entire wall of the chapel facing the door, ranks among Perugino's masterpieces. Painted in 1504, when he was at the height of his powers, and before the achievements of Leonardo, Michelangelo and Raphael had wholly overshadowed his reputation, this fresco represents the fulfilment of the Quattrocento. Perugino has effortlessly mastered the problems of perspective, of anatomy and of composing a large group of figures, all problems that puzzled and intrigued artists of the early Renaissance. In addition, his ability to paint in fresh colours and to capture the softness of the Umbrian landscape surpasses that of any of his contemporaries. Indeed, Perugino was chosen as the leader of the team summoned to Rome by Sixtus IV in the 1480s to paint the walls of the Sistine Chapel, a team that included such high flyers as Botticelli, Ghirlandaio and Signorelli.

Before leaving Città della Pieve, you might like to enjoy one of the landscapes which so inspired Perugino. Following Via dei Bianchi down, bear left and turn left down Via Bacciadonna, reputedly the narrowest street in Italy and an excellent place to improve your knowledge of your fellow travellers (hence the name, which means kiss the woman). The view at the end of the street encompasses the whole valley from Chiusi (ancient Clusium, as in Lars Porsena) across into Tuscany. The *Autostrada del Sole*, the motorway from Rome to Florence, runs straight across the landscape, but amazingly is almost invisible.

If it is a fine day, and you have a picnic in the boot of your car, or want a delightful walk into the countryside, the small Templar chapel set in an olive grove to the south of the town is a truly idyllic spot. The track is rudimentary, with negligible signposts, so either obtain instructions from the Tourist Office in Piazza Matteotti 4, or use your best Italian to ask directions from the locals. If you are over-protective of your car, or it has been raining, and you can't be bothered to walk, forget it. The actual frescoes in the chapel, mostly dating from the thirteenth century, are not particularly good, but the place possesses a remarkably strong atmosphere.

Perugino's 'Martyrdom of St Sebastian' hangs in a little chapel outside Panicale. The 'Madonna', in the Convent of Sant' Agnese, Perugia, is one of his most moving works. It gives the spectator a real sense of discovery.

From Città della Pieve, take the SS220 towards Perugia and, just before Tavernelle, turn off to the left to Panicale. Built of the same red brick as Perugino's home town, Panicale is even more picturesque, with an extraordinarily sophisticated plan for such a minute place. Two concentric streets surround a series of three interconnecting piazzas ascending the hill, giving it a striking similarity to the plan of Siena.

Just to the east of the village stands the chapel of San Sebastiano, overlooking Lake Trasimene. Collect the key from Piazza del Mercato 13 at the foot of the steps to the right of the entrance (the sacristan will be less than amused if you choose to interrupt his extended lunch break, so beware). Even more than in Città della Pieve, there is a tangible sense of discovery as you catch your first glimpse of Perugino's 'Martyrdom of St Sebastian' on the altar wall.

The languid saint, standing in front of a triumphal arch, seems totally unperturbed by the archers who unleash arrows into his body from all angles. The delectable landscape in which the background dissolves into the characteristic Umbrian blue, shows the artist's mastery of aerial perspective. An excuse for Perugino to show off his knowledge of human anatomy, the fresco was actually commissioned as a plague deterrent – St Sebastian was enormously popular all over Europe for his supposed ability to shield people from the plague, the scourge of medieval Europe.

The last Perugino on this route is the most exciting of all. If you have time, take the longer, more scenic, road along the southern shore of Lake Trasimene back to Perugia. Head due north until you reach the lake and turn right on to the SS99. On your left stand the timeless trademarks of the fishermen: nets suspended over the water, posts marking the lake's shallows, and boats ready to embark for the evening's catch. On your right the fields are filled with sunflowers, their heads turned towards the sun.

At Santo Savino head for Magione and join the SS75 bis, which takes you to Perugia. Taking the first exit for Perugia, and bearing left round the city walls, you come to the Porta Sant' Angelo, the north-western entrance to the city, at the beginning of Corso Garibaldi. On your right, 100 metres up the street, stands the fifth-century round church of Sant' Angelo, with its sixteen antique columns, which is one of a few precious survivals throughout Europe. Opposite, across Corso Garibaldi, a small street leads up to the Convento di Sant' Agnese. It seems so insensitive to intrude on the Poor Clares, who live inside, that you need to summon up your courage before ringing the bell.

Opposite: A view of the red brick town of Città della Pieve, the birthplace of Perugino. Right: Perugino's 'Martyrdom of St Sebastian' fills the east end of the little chapel of San Sebastiano outside the village of Panicale. The landscape closely resembles the view from Panicale over Lake Trasimene.

However, the nun who answers the door will be more than happy to give you a glimpse of her charming little garden before taking you to the chapel with its exquisite Perugino. Painted in 1522 for his cousins Verasia and Eustochia as a dowry on their entry into the order, Perugino overcame whatever spiritual qualms he normally suffered from, and produced a work of profound religious emotion. The two donors kneel on either side of the Crowned Madonna, who stands in another sublime Umbrian landscape, just visible beneath layers of dirt, an aesthetic distraction but an excellent preservative. On either side stand St Anthony Abbot and St Anthony of Padua.

Between them, these three Peruginos sum up the most admirable qualities in the artist. You can trawl the world's great art galleries without achieving a deeper insight into the painter than you can gain from one day's travelling through his native landscape, looking at his works in the chapels in which they were painted.

MEDIEVAL PANORAMA

BEVAGNA · MONTEFALCO · ABBEY OF SASSOVIVO · SPELLO

The charming theatrical piazza in Bevagna has two fine Romanesque churches. Don't miss the good Roman mosaics in Via Porta Guelfa.

The church of San Francesco in Montefalco is a treasure house of Umbrian painting. Pride of place goes to Benozzo Gozzoli's delightful frescoes of the Story of St Francis.

Starting-point: Bevagna
Recommended time:
Full day
Length of tour: 22 miles
(35km)
Best time of year: April/June
or September/October
Finishing-point: Spello

Umbria is still wrapped in its medieval past. Not only the main cities, with their cathedrals and palaces, but also the smaller towns, which have scarcely changed since the Middle Ages. St Francis spent most of his career spreading his message in these little borghi; his audiences were townsmen who owned land in the surrounding countryside and thus appreciated his use of imagery of the natural world. The best place to visualize the impact that he and his followers made on central Italy is in towns such as Bevagna, Montefalco and Spello, which have managed to escape the hordes of tourists. In a day's sightseeing, you can visit all three, and make an excursion to the Abbey of Sassovivo, with its glorious cloister.

Bevagna and Montefalco stand like pinnacles on adjoining hills, in an open valley stretching south-west of Foligno. Bevagna, now a forgotten town, was once the seat of the Duchy of Spoleto. Like that of so many Umbrian towns, including Assisi and Todi, the main square, the Piazza Silvestri, stands on the site of the Roman Forum. Two Romanesque churches, both built by the architect Binello in the late twelfth century, face each other across the little piazza, giving it a theatrical quality. One can imagine heralds reading out proclamations from the steps of the Gothic Palazzo dei Consoli, or St Francis preaching to a rapt crowd of nobles, merchants, shopkeepers, bankers, money-lenders and peasants; a typical medieval audience. Indeed it was in Bevagna that he delivered his famous Sermon to the Birds, one of the most charming episodes of the Middle Ages. The façades of the two churches are rather damaged, but the portals contain fine examples of Romanesque sculpture. Inside, both have impressive flights of stairs leading up to the altars.

Bevagna has more to it than meets the eye. The sweeping steps of the Palazzo dei Consoli give little indication of the charming, intimate eighteenth-century theatre inside, which would make a perfect setting for a Goldoni comedy, or a Mozart opera. It is currently under restoration, but you can bluff your way in to see it (or offer the workmen a small 'inducement'). The other site you should not miss is the Roman baths, which have an excellent second-century mosaic of vigorous aquatic life. To reach the baths, head up Corso Matteotti from Piazza Silvestri, turn left into Via Crescimbeni, and take the first left into Via Porta Guelfa. The tritons, seahorses, octopuses and crabs are very realistic.

From Bevagna, a 6km drive to the south-east takes you to the picturesque hill-town of Montefalco which, like Bevagna, prospered under the Duchy of Spoleto. The town possesses a wealth of religious painting. San Fortunato, on the edge of the town, Santa Illuminata, just inside the main gate, and Sant' Agostino, in Corso Mameli, are all filled with Quattrocento frescoes. But if you want to select the best, head for the irregular Piazza del Comune on the crest of the hill and bear left down to the church of San Francesco, a treasure-house of Umbrian and Tuscan painting.

Benozzo Gozzoli's cycle of the Story of St Francis, painted in 1452, was his first fresco cycle, and is one of the most important series of frescoes by a Tuscan painter in Umbria. Here Gozzoli seems effortlessly to have mastered a knowledge of anatomy and perspective: the key lessons of the early Quattrocento. The frescoes possess all the freshness and spontaneity of the early Renaissance. We can perfectly visualize the streets through which St

Francis walked, the Umbrian landscapes with their upright cypresses and spreading fruit trees, the walled city of Arezzo from which the devils flee, and there is a marvellous evocation of the Sermon to the Birds. Gozzoli loved his painting, which is quite apparent in the superb decorative quality of the cycle and the wealth of incidental detail. To the Umbrian painters who flocked to admire these frescoes, they represented something new and exciting, an important advance on the frescoes his Tuscan predecessors had executed on the walls of San Francesco in Assisi. There are plenty more frescoes to admire in the church, particularly Perugino's 'Adoration of the Shepherds', set in a wonderful, spacious, Umbrian landscape.

The abbey of Sassovivo, in the hills above Foligno, possesses a very fine Romanesque cloister.

If you are still thirsting for culture, and can resist the splendid restaurant in Spello a little longer, head north-east to Foligno, badly bombed in the last war. On the eastern side of the town, at the junction of the SS3 and the SS77, a small road winds up through thick oak woods for 6km to the abbey of Sassovivo. It was founded in 1070 by the Benedictines (St Benedict himself came from nearby Norcia – see page 98), and the magnificent cloister was added in 1229. Romanesque in style, with a sequence of double columns with rounded arches marching round the courtyard, it was executed by the Roman Pietro de Maria, who provided variety by introducing pairs of twisted columns to break up the rhythm. There is a real air of peace to this cloister, even though it has been disestablished and there are no monks to be seen. The view from the monastic buildings is amazingly unspoilt, with scarcely a building in sight.

Spello is a perfectly preserved medieval town. Head straight for Pinturicchio's dazzling frescoes in the church of Santa Maria Maggiore.

The last stop on this itinerary is the most charming of all. The little town of Spello rises up the hillside immediately off the SS3 between Foligno and Assisi. It is a perfect survival from the days of Umbria's glory. A car can barely fit through its narrow streets, let alone a coach, which protects it from tourist assaults. To savour the full charm of the place – providing you have a stout pair of shoes – leave your car outside the Roman Porta Venere, and walk straight up the hill, preferably taking the pedestrian route to the left of the main street.

The church of Santa Maria Maggiore stands on the right hand side of Via Cavour opposite a small convent. I once stayed here in a bitter cold March, which I found to be good for the soul, but precious little else. Fortified by faith and the imminent prospect of Easter, the nuns, unlike their guests, obviously had no need for such luxuries as heating or hot water, and I was woken every morning to a dawn chorus of Hallelujahs.

Nevertheless, I was able to enjoy, quite alone, the exquisite frescoes in the church, some of the most beautiful paintings in Umbria. The Cappella Baglioni, in the left aisle, was painted by Pinturicchio (1454-1513) in 1501, immediately after the painter's return from decorating the apartments of the terrifying Borgia family in the Vatican. The splendour of the draperies and the brilliance of the colours create a sumptuous effect, fully justifying Pinturicchio's nickname of rich painter. The scenes represent the Annunciation, the Adoration of the Shepherds and Christ among the Doctors. The rolling Umbrian landscape opens out behind the figures, and Pinturicchio, perhaps having studied Gozzoli in nearby Montefalco, fills the backgrounds with a wealth of incidental detail. Unlike his contemporary Perugino, whose figures live in an idealized world, Pinturicchio's shepherds foreshadow by two generations the Bassanos' interest in genre painting. In the Annunciation scene, you can see a portrait of the artist, which hangs on the wall behind the Virgin.

Opposite: A detail of Pinturicchio's charming 'Adoration of the Shepherds', a masterpiece tucked away in the church of Santa Maria Maggiore in Spello. Top: The Romanesque cloister of the abbey of Sassovivo surrounding an ornate well-head. Bottom: The Palazzo dei Consoli stands in the Piazza Silvestri at Bevagna.

TOUR 15

THE HEART OF THE APENNINES

SPOLETO · NORCIA · PIANO GRANDE · ASCOLI PICENO

Spoleto is one of the most beautiful towns in central Italy. The setting of the Duomo is unsurpassed. Filippo Lippi's frescoes inside have just been restored to their original freshness.

Norcia stands high in the Apennines. The town is full of mementoes to St Benedict, its most famous native son.

Starting-point: Spoleto
Recommended time: Very full day or a day and a half
Length of tour: 79 miles (127km)
Best time of year: May/June for the wild flowers
Finishing-point: Ascoli Piceno

Spoleto makes an ideal starting-point for an excursion into the Apennines. The town stands on a hilltop overlooking a typical Umbrian landscape of rolling hills and picturesque towns and villages, but immediately to the east you ascend into the mountains. The differences can be gauged from comparing Gian Carlo Menotti's Festival of the Two Worlds in Spoleto – a world famous event attended by the beautiful people – with Franco Zeffirelli's setting of his film *Brother Sun, Sister Moon*, an account of the life of St Francis, in the remote Piano Grande, a landscape of lonely grandeur.

Menotti was attracted by Spoleto's picturesque aspect, with its medieval fortress and striking Ponte delle Torri, and excited by the thought of using the Roman amphitheatre for his performances; but he was inspired, above all, by the dramatic possibilities of the long shelving flight of steps leading into the Piazza del Duomo. As in the Campo in Siena, the architect had the originality to place the key building at the bottom, rather than the top of the square, so that the view unfolds as you descend into the piazza. The façade is a mixture of styles, with a Renaissance portico placed beneath a series of medieval rose windows.

If you are coming to a concert and have arrived a little early, you can venture inside the Duomo and admire the superb colours of the Filippo Lippi frescoes of the Life of the Virgin in the apse. Fra Filippo Lippi is an extraordinary mixture: a libertine who managed to paint some of the most beautiful religious works of the Quattrocento, allegedly using his mistress as the model for the Madonna.

The interior of the Duomo, despite the splendour of the Lippi frescoes, is cold and characterless in a typically neoclassical manner. If you want to discover a stronger religious atmosphere, the unadorned church of Sant' Eufemia, on the east side of the piazza, has a simplicity that looks back to the origins of Christianity. This small church, with its Roman columns in the nave, provides a link between the classical world of Marius and Sulla, both of whom tried to capture the town, and the era of the Papal General Cardinal Albornoz in the fourteenth century.

You can better understand Albornoz's achievement in reconquering so much of central Italy for the Papacy when you have wound your way along the mountainous roads through the Apennines into the Marche. From Spoleto, the tortuous SS395 ascends a narrow, claustrophobic valley, covered in ilex and pines. You begin to appreciate what an impenetrable barrier the Apennines have always been, and how, historically, they have cut off the provinces to the east from those to the west.

After 19km, turn left on to the SS209, which brings you into another valley, thickly wooded with a profusion of poplars, acacias, vines, olives and ilex. At Triponzo, after 7km, turn right on to the SS396 to Norcia. The town stands in an open bowl, ringed by hills. Even in this distant outpost of civilization, more famed for its salame and as the birthplace of St Benedict, the founder of monasticism, than for its culture, the layout of the piazza, where the campanili of the two churches and the Palazzo Comunale echo one another, shows the Italian genius for town planning. The statue of the rugged saint stands in the centre of the piazza, where the elegant brick loggia of the palazzo faces the fortified Castellina Vignola. The castle houses a museum, which will be 'in restauro' for some considerable time to come, if the rather pessimistic date of 2025 written beneath the notice-board is anything to go by.

The Basilica of St Benedict, on the right of the palazzo, has a handsome Gothic façade with a rose window over the carved doorway. The crypt dates back to the first century AD, betraying Norcia's Roman origins, and the diamond pattern of the brick-work, known as *opus reticulatum*, is still visible on the walls. This is where St Benedict and his sister St Scholastica were born c.480. The building was converted into an oratory in the sixth century, and subsequently enlarged in the Middle Ages.

Historically, Norcia is famous for its blunt-speaking people, epitomized by the down-to-earth practicality of St Benedict. His Rule, the basis for all religious orders, aimed to bring people closer to God through a practical division of the day into periods of prayer, study and work. The Papacy, needless to say, with its extravagant ceremonies and rituals, regarded St Benedict and his home town of Norcia with grave suspicion. Ironically, one aspect of papal ritual was the singing of the papal choir and the Norcians were required to produce castrati for the choir, a practice that lasted well into the nineteenth century. The last castrato died as recently as 1913, and the sign outside a butcher's shop in a nearby village, stating '*Oggi Castrato*' (today castration) – a novel way to attract customers – is enough to induce a hasty retreat, discretion being undoubtedly the better part of valour.

From Norcia, head south and, after 2km, take the small side road on the left which climbs sharply out of the valley. When you finally crest the ridge, you suddenly find yourself in the Piano Grande, a vast open bowl set in the mountains. A smattering of sheep and goats, and the road lifting towards the distant village of Castelluccio, are the only indications of the presence of humanity. In spring and early summer the wild flowers form a multi-coloured carpet of bright reds, yellows and blues. Take the road to the left to Castelluccio and bear right just before the village. This is border country. The Marche lies on the eastern side of the

Piano Grande. After 6km a road to the right leads down to Arquata, from where the SS4 follows the River Tronto down for some 29km to Ascoli Piceno.

Ascoli Piceno is, in my opinion, the most under-rated town in central Italy. It is a city of travertine (a white limestone), one of the most handsome of all building materials, unlike the other towns of the Marche, and of the neighbouring Emilia-Romagna, which are constructed in brick, because of the shortage of stone quarries. Consequently, even the most humdrum church or palace assumes a genuine refinement.

Sightseeing in Ascoli is a haphazard activity. It is easy to become muddled by the number of churches constructed of unornamented blocks of travertine. Even more confusing is the way that buildings are situated in the middle of the road, so that the traffic swirls around the church of Santi Vincenzo e Anastasio, the Baptistery, which is thus divorced from the Duomo, and the campanile of Santa Maria inter Vineas, oblivious to their artistic merit.

The Piazza dell' Arringo, in front of the Duomo, is similarly wrecked by being used as a car-park. This is doubly unfortunate, because Dell' Amatrice's handsome façade possesses the best proportions of any in the city. Cola dell' Amatrice is Ascoli's most famous artist, a typical Renaissance man who could turn his hand to painting or architecture at will. He liked to add classical elements to the traditional blank stone wall favoured by the architects of Ascoli. On the Duomo façade he included four columns, niches, two thrones and an entablature to break up the solid mass of masonry.

The interior, in complete contrast, is a hotchpotch of nineteenth-century frescoes, modern stained glass, scalloped niches and Murano chandeliers, more suited to a Venetian ballroom. In this curious setting one scarcely expects to find, in a chapel off the right aisle, one of the greatest paintings in the Marche. Carlo Crivelli, Dell' Amatrice's master in painting, although always conscious of his

Ascoli Piceno is a real find. All the most important buildings are constructed of travertine, the most handsome of all building materials.

The Piano Grande is a supremely beautiful bowl in the heart of the mountains. Try to visit it when the wild flowers are out in June.

Opposite: The dramatic Ponte degli Torri at Spoleto with the church of San Pietro appearing through the arch on the right. <u>Right:</u> Early morning light touches the travertine façades of the Palazzo Capitano del Popolo and the church of San Francesco in the Piazza del Popolo in Ascoli Piceno.

Venetian heritage, chose to live in the Marche for the last three decades of his life.

Crivelli's masterpiece, a powerful polyptych depicting the Madonna and Child with attendant saints, hangs in the Chapel of the Sacrament off the right of the nave. Set in a fine Gothic frame, the saints, with their spiky drapery and attenuated hands and feet, placed against a gold background, possess great emotional intensity and power as they gather around the Madonna and Child, seated on a grand, sculptural throne with dolphin arm rests. The quality of this painting far surpasses anything hanging in the Pinacoteca in the Palazzo Comunale off the piazza, apart from a beautiful cope given by Pope Nicholas IV to the Duomo in 1288. The picture collection, despite its list of big names (Titian, Luca Giordano, Guido Reni, Ribera, Bellotto and, surprisingly, Turner), is not of very high quality.

When you have toured the sights, the best place to relax in Ascoli is the Piazza del Popolo, which is lined by a series of modern brick arcades surmounted by elegant windows and swallow tail battlements. Each arch faces a shop front and was paid for by the shopkeeper. Human nature being what it is, no two shopkeepers could agree on the price of an arch, and so they all vary in width, and yet such is the Italian genius for town planning, that the overall effect is very harmonious. The piazza is centred on the gleaming white façade of the Palazzo Capitano del Popolo, which echoes the travertine pavement. The side façade of the church of San Francesco forms the north end of the square. The loggia, on the far side of the church, is used for a colourful fruit and flower market, where the women, as always in Mediterranean countries (and, some would say, elsewhere too), do all the work, while the men sit around gossiping.

TOUR 16

PRINCELY SPLENDOUR

URBINO · SAN LEO · URBANIA

Urbino has remained totally unspoilt. Federico da Montefeltro's magnificent Ducal Palace is among the outstanding buildings of the Quattrocento. It possesses paintings by Piero della Francesca and Raphael.

Federico da Montefeltro (1422-82), soldier, scholar and lavish patron of the arts, personifies the Italian Quattrocento. The role model of the enlightened *condottiere*, the inspiration of his troops and citizens alike, he dominated the small city-state of Urbino through sheer force of personality. Artists of the calibre of Piero della Francesca, Alberti and Uccello, as well as Justus van Ghent from Flanders and Pedro Berruguete from Spain, flocked to his court, and princes from all over Italy sent their sons to learn the martial arts and complete their education at his feet. The image of the aging warrior, with his famous hawk-like profile and drooping eye, sitting in his loggia, enjoying the view over his beloved Marche, while a courtier reads out his favourite passages from Livy, evokes this profoundly civilized world.

The Italy of the later fifteenth century was riven by feuds and rivalries between the city-states. In a society where warfare was endemic, and vividly depicted by Uccello, with his comical knights on rocking-horses, the *condottiere*, or mercenary leader, was the kingmaker. Federico da Montefeltro was an outstanding *condottiere*, and profited from his campaigns to extend his duchy to include the whole of the northern Marche. With his new-found wealth, he indulged his love of the arts, based on a study of antiquity, to the full, building a series of palaces and fortresses, commissioning paintings, sculpture and tapestries, and forming a magnificent library, the greatest of its era. Federico's capital at Urbino is worth a whole day's sightseeing, but if you prefer to concentrate on the Ducal Palace, you will also have time to make an excursion to Urbania and on to the Montefeltro fortress of San Leo.

The building that most closely summarizes Federico's aspirations is the Ducal Palace in Urbino. It reflects the humanistic ideals of an era in which man felt himself to be the master of all things. This is apparent in the desire for knowledge shared by all the leading artists attracted to his court. The architectural treatises of Alberti and Francesco di Giorgio Martini, the 'Ideal City' attributed to Luciano Laurana which so influenced the young Bramante, the experiments in perspective of Piero della Francesca, and the subtlety of the *trompe-l'oeil* intarsia work in Federico's Studiolo, or study, all betray a high intellectual curiosity.

The architectural history of the palace is rather confused, but the presiding genius, responsible for the overall plan, and the entrance court, was almost certainly the Dalmatian Luciano Laurana, who began work in 1467-8, while Francesco di Giorgio was responsible for the details, including the exquisite modelling of the windows. The main façade, with holes for scaffolding still visible, is unfinished apart from a few beautiful pieces of marble. The most unforgettable image of the palace can only be seen from the far side of the town, where Laurana's triple loggia, set between two cylindrical towers capped with pinnacles, appears like the setting of a fairy-tale.

The entrance to the palace is through a beautiful courtyard, with a harmonious arcade running around the ground floor, and an inscription on a frieze above celebrating the merits of Federico's enlightened rule. The picture collection is housed upstairs in a fine suite of rooms, designed by Francesco di Giorgio. The fascination of these rooms, and to my mind perhaps the greatest charm of the palace, lies in the subtlety of the carving of the doorways, fireplaces and cornices, by Ambrogio Barocci and his pupils, where similar motifs are used, but with slight vari-

Starting-point: Urbino

Recommended time:

Very full day

Length of tour: 40 miles

(65km)

Best time of year: May/June

or September/October

Finishing-point: Urbania

ations as in a Bach fugue, so that you can spend hours admiring the endless inventiveness in the different rooms. This applies even to the window seats, which are extremely elegant. The Duke's arms, with the Montefeltro eagle and the bursting bomb, resembling a monstrous jellyfish, appear everywhere. The finest carving is on the fireplace in the Sala degli Angeli, by Domenico Rosselli, which ranks with the famous Cantorie by Donatello and Luca della Robbia in Florence.

English visitors will be surprised to recognize the recurring motif of the Garter, which reflects Federico's pride in being appointed a knight of the order by Edward IV in 1474, the same year that Pope Sixtus IV made him a Duke. His invalid son Guidobaldo, an equally civilized ruler, and so popular with his subjects that they rose up in insurrection when he was deposed by Cesare Borgia, was to receive the same honour from Henry VII.

The most intimate room in the palace is Federico's Studiolo, probably designed by Botticelli and Francesco di Giorgio, where the realism of the intarsia work, with books and lutes precariously perched on the edge of half-open doors of cupboards, and the Garter hanging out of a drawer, makes it appear as though we are intruding on the Duke in his studies. The objects depicted reflect the wide variety of Federico's interests. He has hung up his suit of armour in order to concentrate on his intellectual pursuits: books alternating with astrolabes and musical instruments. In the centre, a charming squirrel chews a nut before a distant view of Urbino. To emphasize his own status, Federico had portraits, now mostly hanging in the Louvre, of philosophers, prophets and his illustrious contemporaries, painted by Justus van Ghent and Pedro Berruguete above the wooden panels.

The paintings and the sculpture in the collection proclaim the cultural achievement of Federico and his successors. Francesco di Giorgio's head of the Duke's wife, Battista Sforza, and Agostino di Duccio's lyrical head of the Madonna stand out among the busts and reliefs. The two most famous paintings are by Piero della Francesca, whose reputation has soared like a rocket. The 'Flagellation', with its enigmatic composition, and brilliant jewel-like colours, showing the influence of early Flemish painting, is strangely compelling. The curious dichotomy between the two halves of the composition and the lack of concern of the three figures in the foreground for the events in the palace behind them, have defied the most intense analysis. Piero would doubtless have laughed at the extraordinary tortured logic used by art historians to identify the foreground figures and to decipher the complexities of perspective. Piero's 'Madonna di Senigallia', is one of his last works. The light is cooler, the figures are more severe, but the colours, especially the Virgin's rose-red dress, are as beautiful as ever.

The scope of Federico's collection is well represented in the following rooms which overlook the Duke's hanging garden. Federico himself appears twice, in the splendid portrait by Pedro Berruguete of him seated in his study with his son, proudly showing off the Order of the Garter on his left leg, and in Justus van Ghent's damaged 'Communion of the Apostles' in the adjoining Sala degli Angeli, where he is depicted talking to the Persian ambassador. Elsewhere, Uccello's predella panels of the Miracle of the Profanation of the Host, a beautiful but faded Madonna and Child attributed to Verocchio, and a superb Ideal City, possibly by Laurana, testify to Federico's discerning taste. The Ideal City, which has also been attributed to Piero, possesses an almost spiritual feel in the loving care which the artist has bestowed on the most beautiful buildings that he could visualize for his architectural Utopia.

The ducal court continued to flourish after Federico's death in 1482. His son Guidobaldo was equally devoted to the arts, creating a flourishing maiolica industry and patronizing the young Raphael, whose father was court painter. The palace possesses one work by him, a sensitive portrait, 'La Muta' (the silent one), who transfixes the spectator

<u>Opposite:</u> A romantic view of the triple loggia of the Ducal Palace at Urbino, designed by Luciano Laurana for Federico da Montefeltro. <u>Left:</u> The mountain fortress of San Leo is perched dramatically on the rim of a cliff.

The mountain fortress of San Leo is in a spectacular site. Francesco di Giorgio's fort dominates the view for miles around.

with her gaze. Raphael became a great friend of Baldassare Castiglione, whom he met in Urbino, and who was so impressed by Guidobaldo's artistic and literary court that he immortalized it in *The Courtier*, which became the manual for civilized behaviour all over Europe. Urbino remained an artistic centre, although of dwindling importance, throughout the sixteenth century, and the second floor of the Ducal Palace is devoted to the works of Federico Barocci (1526-1612), the last major painter born in the town.

There is nothing to rival the Ducal Palace in the town of Urbino, but two of Barocci's brilliantly coloured masterpieces hang in the cold, neoclassical Duomo. The complex poses of the figures in the 'St Sebastian', and the interest in the genre aspects of 'The Last Supper', in which much care is devoted to the servants handing out the food and drink, look forward to baroque art. Before leaving the town, you might like to glance at Raphael's house in Via Raffaello, and at two oratories in Via Mazzini. The Oratorio di San Giuseppe contains Federico Brandini's extraordinarily realistic depiction of the Nativity in stucco, while the Oratorio di San Giovanni, at the end of the street, is filled with frescoes by the Salimbeni brothers, typical of the flamboyant International Gothic style of the early fifteenth century. The scenes of the Life of the Baptist are peopled with the citizens of Urbino dressed in all their finery. Notice the comical way that saints Zacharias and Elizabeth, the Baptist's parents, are given square haloes.

Despite the grandeur of the Ducal Palace, Urbino is still a provincial town, sheltered from the developments which have ruined so much of the coastline. Washing hangs from the terracotta tile roofs as it does in towns and villages all over Italy. The view from the palace into the countryside has scarcely changed from the time of Federico.

Just beyond the town walls, on the road to Pesaro, the simple brick Oratorio di San Bernardino stands in a grove of cypresses. The chapel houses the tombs of Federico and his son Guidobaldo, facing each other across the nave. As in his masterpiece in

Cortona (see page 42), the architect Francesco di Giorgio picked out the windows and entablature in stone to provide a minimum of decoration. It is very probable that Piero's great painting of Federico kneeling before the Madonna and Saints (now in the Brera in Milan) originally hung in the crossing. From the chapel you can enjoy a wonderful view back across the vineyards and wheat fields to Urbino.

In contrast to the refinement of the Ducal Palace of Urbino, the fortress of San Leo, guarding the northern flank of Federico's duchy, situated on an impregnable site in the mountains, emphasizes the military achievements of Federico. The approach is enough to put off any invading army, and helps to explain how the neighbouring republic of San Marino managed to retain its independence through the centuries. If you head due north from Urbania, you go through a patchwork of fields of wheat, vines, maize and grass. After 21km you pass Sassocorvaro, beside a little lake, dominated by the immense walls of another Montefeltro fortress built by the ubiquitous Francesco di Giorgio. The countryside gradually becomes more arid, as you ascend into the mountains, with thick oak woods interspersed with hillsides covered in broom. Following the bed of a small stream for 5km north-west, turn left at Macerata, and then right after 7km at Caturchio. The landscape becomes increasingly dramatic, with stupendous views to the south and east. Eventually you glimpse, in the distance, the spectacular rocky eyrie of San Leo.

San Leo is in a truly magnificent position, set on the extremity of a precipice like the bow of a ship. On a fine day, with the northern Marche at your feet and San Marino in the far distance, you can almost see right to the Adriatic. San Leo's history is a microcosm of that of Italy. Inhabited by the Romans, the citadel was taken and retaken by Goths, Byzantines, Lombards and Franks before enjoying a moment of glory as the capital of Italy under Berengar II in AD962-4. San Leo later played host to St Francis, who preached

Urbania has another palace built for Federico da Montefeltro.

a sermon in the piazza in 1213, greatly impressing Dante, who subsequently described the event in the *Purgatorio*.

The town was put on the map by Monfeltrano I (1132-1203), the founder of the Montefeltro dynasty, and the father of Bonconte da Montefeltro, who was given the county of Urbino by the Holy Roman Emperor Frederick II in 1234. After it had been seized successively by the Church and the Malatestas of Rimini, Federico da Montefeltro earned his military spurs by scaling the supposedly impregnable walls of the citadel at the head of his men in 1441. With some difficulty, the Montefeltri and their della Rovere successors held on to the fortress until 1631, when it passed to the Papacy, who used it as a prison for political prisoners. The two most illustrious inmates were the infamous alchemist and necromancer Count Cagliostro, who died in a cell here in 1795, and Felice Orsini, a hero of the Risorgimento, who was incarcerated here in 1844. Orsini ended his revolutionary career in front of a firing squad in Paris after attempting to blow up Napoleon III.

The fort itself dates back to Roman times, but was altered and greatly strengthened by Francesco di Giorgio for Federico in 1473. Niccolò Machiavelli, an expert on Renaissance warfare, praised it as a perfect example of a military fortress. You can still visit the cells in which Cagliostro and Orsini were confined.

There are two handsome Romanesque churches in the town: the simple eleventh century parish church of Santa Maria Assunta, known as the Pieve, whose columns are taken from the original Roman temple which stood on the site, and the more sophisticated and slightly later Duomo, with its elegant Renaissance balustrade dividing the raised choir from the nave, which was designed to house pilgrims who came to worship the body of San Leo. These churches, together with the fortress and the splendour of the landscape, stretching away in every direction, make San Leo one of the most attractive, as well as one of the most dramatic, sites in the Marche.

By now you will probably have had enough sightseeing for one day, but if you want to make a slight detour on the way back to Urbino, or, alternatively, would like to make a separate excursion, you can head south through the mountains to the little town of Urbania, which lies some 17km due west of Urbino. This is Urbino on a more intimate scale and on a less spectacular site. The town is wedged into the bend of the River Metauro, giving constant views through the trees and across the vegetable patches down to the fishermen casting their lines at the water's edge.

A series of arcaded streets surround the modest brick exterior of the Ducal Palace, with a loggia on the upper floor overlooking the river. Inside, a staircase off the simple but elegant courtyard, built by Francesco di Giorgio, leads up to the Museum of Ceramics, with its maiolica pots, for which Urbania, like Urbino, was famous, and the Library, where there is a permanent exhibition of drawings and prints from the era of the Montefeltri, many of them by Federico Barocci. Such was Federico's passion for building that he had another hunting lodge constructed at Il Barco, just outside the town, which he preferred to the Ducal Palace. Urbania has rather mournful associations with the Montefeltro family. Originally named Castel Durante, its name was changed in 1636 in honour of Pope Urban VIII, shortly after the auction of all the remaining Montefeltri possessions that had not already been removed to Florence.

The two palaces at Urbino and Urbania, together with the fortress at San Leo, display the diversity of Federico da Montefeltro's achievement, both as an enlightened patron of the arts, and a successful *condottiere*. By Federico's death in 1482, Urbino had become one of the most famous towns in all Europe. For those who wish to seek further evidence of his genius, the Ducal Palace in the attractive medieval town of Gubbio, although now sadly denuded of its former glory, lies just over the border in Umbria.

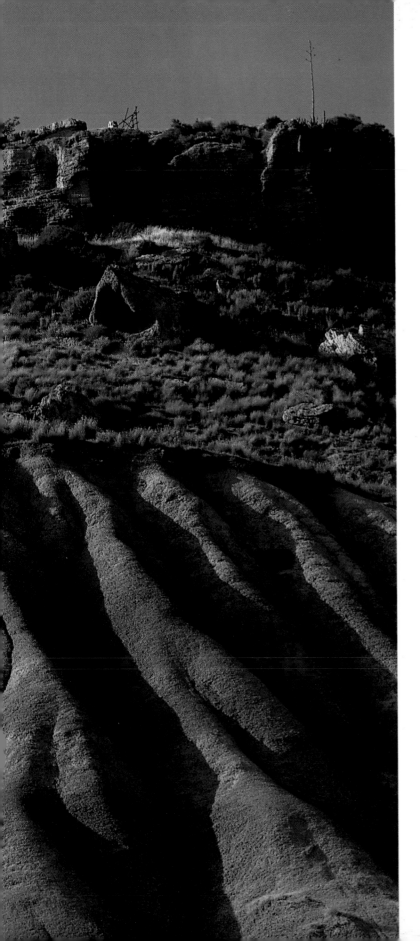

SICILY

To visit the island of Sicily is to experience the living past. This is equally apparent in its art and in the lifestyle of its inhabitants. To enter the Duomo in Syracuse, where the Doric columns of the ancient Greek temple are still visible, is to be transported back to the world of Plato and Archimedes. Goethe, on his epic visit in 1787, instinctively began thumbing through his favourite copy of the *Odyssey*. The strength of Sicilian traditions, particularly religious traditions, with their regional peculiarities, is rooted in a pre-Christian world which is still taken very seriously. You can experience this living past, where nothing has changed for centuries, throughout the island: in the sounds and smells of the fish market drifting through the doorway of the Duomo in Catania, in the itinerant street vendor hawking his wares in the early morning in Palermo like some secular muezzin, in the Easter festivals which vary from village to village in the mountainous interior, and in the old women fanning themselves as they recite the Rosary on a hot summer's evening before an image of the Madonna.

Sicily has suffered a tumultuous history. More than a province but less than a country, lying at a vital strategic position, and blessed with a fertile soil and a benevolent climate that has earned it the title of garden of the Mediterranean, it has rarely enjoyed any peace. Waves of invaders – Carthaginians, Greeks, Romans, Byzantines, Arabs, Normans, Angevins and Aragonese – have disputed suzerainty, giving the Sicilians a fatalistic acceptance of their fate. This has been augmented by the succession of earthquakes and eruptions of Mount Etna which have devastated the island. The numerous invasions and natural calamities have strongly influenced the Sicilian character. Less loquacious and more restrained than the Neapolitan, with whom he is often compared, the Sicilian possesses an implacable resolution.

Sicilian mythology reflects the violence of the island's history. The Rape of Persephone in the fields of Enna, the sword suspended by a horsehair over the head of Damocles, the whirlpool of Charybdis, into which Odysseus was almost sucked, and the giant Enceladus chained beneath Mount Etna, are all legends that possess a primeval savagery. This is equally true of the mythology surrounding the Mafia, whose perverted code of honour and ferocious system of discipline and initiation rites hark back, as Norman Lewis persuasively argues in *The Honoured Society*, to the tribal customs of the Bronze Age.

Part of Sicily's appeal is this interweaving of past and present. The fact that the bandit Giuliano used the Archbishop's Palace at Monreale in the 1950s for many of his meetings with figures of authority, and the recent theft of the body of St Lucy from the Duomo in Syracuse, greatly increase the interest of these buildings. To appreciate Sicily to the full, you need to emulate the fatalism of the locals. Try not to be driven demented by the scaffolding that envelops so many of the finest buildings, ignore the ruined coastline, and take a philosophical view of opening times, churches and museums *in restauro*, and of locals whose favourite time to check the exhaust pipe of their scooters is at three o'clock in the morning.

This section of the book emphasizes the unique qualities of Sicily's art and landscape. I have concentrated on the three most original artistic styles: Greek, Norman and baroque, each of which testifies to the island's cosmopolitan history. The masterpieces of these three styles are scattered throughout the island, but are accessible, enabling you to enjoy the natural grandeur of the countryside. They are linked by the Sicilian genius, probably inherited from the Greeks, for placing a building in the landscape. The temples of Segesta, Selinunte and Agrigento, the cathedral at Cefalù and the churches of Gagliardi are all set in the most superb positions.

Many of the most interesting sites lie in and around Palermo, and this is the most sensible base for a three-day introduction to the island, although you need at least a week to begin to appreciate the depth of Sicily's culture. The first two routes in this section use Palermo as a starting-point. But before embarking on the first of these, to the great Norman cathedrals, you should see the Cappella Palatina in the Palazzo dei Normanni, King Roger II's private chapel, a superb ensemble of glistening mosaics, precious marbles and a stalactite ceiling.

Built in 1132-40, the chapel is one of the earliest and most sumptuous examples of the Norman-Saracenic style, a fusion of the Latin, Greek and Arab civilizations. The complex wooden ceiling, with its inscription in Arabic glorifying Roger, is purely Islamic in inspiration, rivalling in complexity that of the Mihrab in the Mezquita in Cordoba. The superbly coloured mosaics were executed by Byzantine craftsmen, so that the Archangels in the dome appear like a gorgeously attired Imperial Guard beneath the figure of Christ. Maupassant captured the fairy-tale quality of the chapel when he described it as 'the most astonishing jewel of which the human mind may dream'.

Just to the south of the Palazzo dei Normanni, in Via dei Benedettini, stands the charming little cloistered garden of San Giovanni degli Eremiti. Although this oasis can be inundated with locals celebrating a wedding, or foreigners looking for the perfect photo-opportunity, it remains an idyllic spot to escape from the traffic which is one of the banes of Palermo. The city possesses any number of fine baroque churches, decorated with the traditional Sicilian *marmi mischi* (fragments of crushed marble forming ornamental patterns), but these churches need to be visited during a service, when the splendour of the Catholic liturgy, with its music and incense, bring the richness of the gold and the host of paintings and sculptures to life. Elsewhere the Archaeological Museum possesses the greatest classical sculpture in the island in the metopes from the temples at Selinunte.

But if you want to carry away a single image of perfection, go to see Antonello da Messina's exquisite 'Annunciation', which hangs in a small room on the first floor of the Galleria Regionale. The beauty of the Madonna's face, her introverted smile seeming to suggest thoughts beyond our comprehension, and the simplicity of the gesture of her outstretched right hand, combine the idealism of the Italian Renaissance with the intimacy of Flemish art. Antonello managed to capture the perfect stillness of one of the most profound moments in Christianity. From my experience, there are no more than a handful of paintings in western art which command such a strong reaction from the spectator.

Having visited Palermo, the best way to see Sicily is to tour the island, stopping at two or three sites en route. A logical way to do this is to follow my final three itineraries, basing yourself in Agrigento and Syracuse, from where you can explore the Greek temples and the baroque towns of the south-east. A final stopping-point is Taormina, a suitable place to relax if you are suffering from an excess of culture. The town still retains some of the charm which made it such a popular resort at the beginning of the century, when D.H. Lawrence wrote purple passages about the beauty of Mount Etna, while others sampled the beauty of the young male inhabitants.

The view of Mount Etna from the Greek Theatre still takes your breath away, particularly when the summit is covered in snow. You can visit the volcano from Taormina, but this is not an expedition for the faint-hearted, and takes you through fertile fields and groves of fruit trees into a strange, barren, lunar landscape. Etna is the most active volcano in Europe, and its frequent, violent eruptions have periodically devastated this part of the island. In 396BC the lava reached the sea, and in 1669 it flowed through Catania, some 30km away, and 2km beyond the city into the sea. Efforts to prevent or deter the wrath of the mountain rarely succeed, and in the spring of 1992 the flow of lava reached the outskirts of Zefferana Etnea. The Sicilian whose house was about to be consumed adopted a typically philosophical approach, leaving a bottle of wine on his doorstep to appease the gods. The hinterland behind Etna is the wildest and most remote part of Sicily. A series of fortified hill-towns with superb views of the mountain testify to its lawless past. The old traditions have lasted longer here than elsewhere, and, if you enjoy local festivals, there is any number to choose from, particularly during Holy Week.

A tour through the island helps to explain how Sicilian culture has thrived on the waves of invaders. The sheer variety of civilizations far surpasses that of any other Mediterranean island, and has inspired each new racial component. The Romans looked to the Greeks for artistic inspiration, just as the Normans integrated elements of the Byzantine and Arab cultures that preceded them. Goethe claimed that Sicily held the key to an understanding of Italy, and the island certainly seems to possess in extreme forms the aspects of Italy that both attract and repel visitors. The easy acceptance of its artistic masterpieces, and the colour and excitement of markets and festivals, are likely to appeal to anyone who has succumbed to the lure of Italy. On the other hand, the inability of the government to restore the palaces of Palermo, the ruination of the coastline, and the difficulty of visiting the lesser sites, can drive even the most enthusiastic tourist to distraction.

POWER AND OPULENCE

MONREALE · LA MARTORANA · CEFALU · SANTO SPIRITO

Monreale is one of the great medieval cathedrals of Europe. Especially notable for its mosaics. Don't miss the cloister, with its wealth of carved capitals.

The intimacy of the Cappella Palatina, designed for Roger II's private worship and never intended for public viewing, contrasts with the great set pieces of Norman architecture, the cathedrals of Monreale and Cefalù, both of which lie within easy reach of Palermo. I suggest a visit to Monreale first, since there is much more to see, and I find that sightseeing is very much easier in the morning, when everything is guaranteed to be open, even in Sicily, and you can take in more. Cefalù, on the other hand, is a fishing port which needs to be appreciated at leisure over a dish of grilled swordfish. I have included two smaller Norman churches in Palermo, La´ Martorana and Santo Spirito. The former involves a small detour en route from Monreale to Cefalù, and its intimate nature makes a good contrast with the size of the great cathedrals. The latter, closer in style to English Norman architecture, is for the devotee of Sicilian history, or for those who enjoy visiting churches when they are sure that they will only encounter locals carrying out their devotions. Monreale, La Martorana and maybe even Santo Spirito can easily be seen in a morning, leaving the afternoon for Cefalù. If you run out of time, save Santo Spirito for a return trip to Palermo, perhaps combining it with the Cappella Palatina.

In the harsh, volcanic landscape of Sicily, where mountains sheer up like knife edges, and where the laws of order and justice which we take for granted have no application, it comes as a shock to find that the supreme achievements of Sicilian culture (in my view surpassing even the glories of its Greek temples and baroque churches), are the buildings erected by the Normans. Our limited knowledge of history, focusing on the date 1066, tends to omit the fact that, while William and his knights were conquering

England, their compatriots under Robert and Roger de Hauteville were subduing the Arabs in Sicily.

The achievement of Norman architecture in Sicily is particularly fascinating to an Englishman born and brought up within sight of his Norman village church. The sturdy round arches marching solemnly up the nave, the thickness of the walls that have survived unscathed for a thousand years, and the simplicity of the decoration, touch a chord that no other style of architecture can equal.

The shock is therefore all the greater when we enter the Norman churches of Sicily and find ourselves transported into a world of Oriental splendour. The Normans were a highly ambitious and successful race, venturing as far afield as Russia and Constantinople. Their leaders were great warriors and builders, and in Sicily they were prepared to assimilate much of the Arab and Byzantine civilizations that preceded them. Indeed, with their harems filled with eunuchs and beautiful, exotic women, and an autocratic concept of kingship based on the absolutism of the Byzantine emperors, these Norman kings willingly succumbed to the allure of the east.

Yet the Hautevilles retained close connections with their English cousins, and it is therefore not surprising that many of the leading advisers of the Norman kings in Sicily were Englishmen, including Roger II's chancellor, Robert of Selby, and Richard Palmer, Archbishop of Messina. The most romantic connection between the two countries occurred in 1177 when Richard Coeur de Lion's sister Joanna married William the Good and was crowned Queen of Sicily in the splendour of the Palatine Chapel in Palermo. It is this combination of the familiar with the exotic which gives the Norman art in Sicily its unique appeal.

Starting-point: Monreale
Recommended time: Very full day or a day and a half
Length of tour: 105 miles (170km)
Best time of year: Avoid mid-summer
Finishing-point: Palermo (unless you decide to stay overnight in Cefalù)

In 1170 William fell asleep while lying under a carob tree on the royal mountain (Monreale) overlooking Palermo and dreamt that the Virgin showed him where the gold hidden by his father William I (the Bad) lay. With this wealth he proceeded to build a cathedral and a Benedictine monastery on the site in record time between 1172 and 1176. The cathedral at Monreale remains the foremost Norman building in Sicily and one of the wonders of the Middle Ages.

A fortified structure on the outside, the interior is a glorious mixture of mosaics, porphyry and cipollino, with Egyptian granite columns and an intricate marble pavement. Pride of place goes to the glittering gold of the mosaics, which rival any in Ravenna, Venice, Rome or Constantinople. The mosaicists exploited the full possibilities of the medium: coloured glass of every hue is juxtaposed with gold to create a harmony of colour and light and the gold tesserae are set at different angles so that the light is reflected from one surface to another. In an astonishing burst of creativity they were completed within a decade and, such is the durability of mosaic decoration, they are as fresh today as when the artists put the final pieces in place in 1182.

The scenes are designed to be read like an illuminated bible. To the illiterate Sicilian peasant, scratching his living from the soil, they must have appeared like the visual representation of the glory of God. Even to the sophisticated visitor today the experience is overwhelming. It is known that artists from as far afield as Constantinople, North Africa, Provence, Venice, and Naples worked here, although the majority of the work is thought to have been carried out by Sicilian and Venetian craftsmen. The genius in charge remains anonymous to this day.

The stories from Genesis read clockwise round the nave from the chancel. The vivid imagination of the artists brings the scenes to life, whether it is Adam and Eve in their hair shirts being expelled from Eden, Esau returning from a hunting expedition to learn of his lost inheritance, Noah and his wife releasing the animals from the Ark, or the marvellous image of God resting after completing the Creation. The mosaics are also a severe test of one's memory of the Old Testament. Did Abraham really give the angels pork to eat after he learnt that Sarah was with child? And who on earth is the little red figure demanding vengeance after Abel was slain by Cain? (Apparently Abel's Blood.)

The walls of the aisles and the side apses are covered with mosaics of Christ's Ministry and Passion, and the lives of the Apostles. Once again it is the simplicity and realism of the scenes that strike the spectator. There is an immediacy to the cripple picking up his bed and walking, and to the Raising of Lazarus, with the attendants desperately holding their noses, which is completely convincing. Perhaps the finest mosaic is the Resurrection, where the Angel gestures eloquently to the empty tomb.

The apse is dominated by the superb image of Christ Pantocrator, his right hand raised in an act of benediction. Below him Archangels and saints surround the Virgin and Child, including St Thomas à Becket, who was martyred in Canterbury Cathedral in 1170 (Henry II of England was William II's father-in-law). Don't miss two fascinating images, resplendent with gold, on either side of the choir: on the left William II is crowned directly by Christ (a deliberate snub to the Pope, whose duty this should have been), and on the right William dedicates the cathedral to the Virgin (the actual image of the building still, at this stage, fairly crude). In the right apse stand the fine Renaissance tomb of William II, and the handsome porphyry one of his father William I.

The splendour of these mosaics, executed over a century before Giotto and Duccio, help to put the Tuscan artists' importance in perspective. When we read of Giotto's role as a radical innovator, it is as well to remember that, although he was working in a different medium (fresco being the poor man's equivalent of mosaic), he was continuing in a tradition that had been one of the glories of European art for centuries. Indeed, the achievements of the

Opposite: The exotic splendour of Norman Sicily is clearly evident in the King's Fountain in the cloister at Monreale.
Right: The position of Roger II's magnificent cathedral at Cefalù is a typical example of the Sicilian genius for placing a building in the landscape.

mosaicists at Monreale, working in a much more intractable material than fresco, make this building quite the equal of the Arena Chapel in Padua.

Contemporary with the mosaics, though less easy to see, are the bronze doors by Bonnano da Pisa (1185), set behind an eighteenth-century portal, which you pass en route to the cloister. They depict scenes from the Old and New Testaments. Some of the scenes seem quite comical, as when Adam reclines on the ground with his hand behind his head in 'The Creation of Eve', and the lid of the tomb crushes the heads of the Norman guards in 'The Resurrection'. As with so much of the best Romanesque sculpture, Bonnano was at his most inspired in carving the fanciful lions and griffins at the bottom of the doors.

The cloister makes a perfect contrast to the acres of mosaics inside the cathedral. In its exotic garden setting, where poppies and cacti mix freely with roses and palm trees, the sculptors felt free to indulge in a wealth of naturalistic carving, particularly in the columns at the corners of the King's Fountain, where they overflow with an abundance of life. The religious scenes are swamped by lions and peacocks, workers gathering vines and a riot of foliage. The sculpture is typical of the Romanesque of western Europe, but, once again, the introduction of coloured glass and mosaic adds an Oriental element. This exoticism is equally apparent on the exterior of the triple apse of the cathedral. The interlocking arches, with their roundels and columns, are Arabic in inspiration, emphasizing Sicily's trading links with North Africa and Muslim Spain, and its importance as a base for Crusaders stopping off on their way to the Holy Land.

Remarkably, despite the influx of tourists, the town of Monreale has retained its local atmosphere. The old men gossiping beside the fountain in the piazza, the horseman riding down the main street oblivious of the traffic, and the little children marching in front of the town band, are all sights that one could meet in any Sicilian town.

The road from Monreale descends the hillside into Palermo, through Charles V's Triumphal Arch, celebrating the Emperor's victory in Tunis in 1535, past the cathedral to the Quattro Canti, with its four fountains and four statues of the seasons, four kings of Spain and the four patron saints of the city. This is the heart of Palermo, where the four main quarters meet, making it a landmark in baroque town planning. If you turn right down Via Maqueda, you pass, almost immediately on your left, the triple red domes of San Cataldo, with the church of La Martorana directly behind, and the excellent Pizzeria Bellini beside it, should you want to relax for a moment before embarking on more culture.

The church of Santa Maria dell' Ammiraglio, known as La Martorana, was founded by Roger II's Admiral George of Antioch in 1143 (the word admiral comes from the Arab emir, or ruler, and did not originally have any nautical connotations). The Martorana was built by Greek craftsmen on the plan of an Arab mosque, reflecting the extraordinary cosmopolitan quality of the Norman kingdom. Despite the alterations carried out to the façade in the sixteenth century, and the baroque frescoes in the nave, the human scale of the interior and the splendour of the mosaics make this one of the most evocative Norman churches in Sicily. Indeed, the ornateness of the seventeenth-century decoration pales into insignificance compared with the rich colours of the mosaics and the deep reds and greens of the porphyry and verd antique of the Cosmatesque pavement.

The mosaics belong to the world of Byzantium. The Archangels in the dome, robed like soldiers of the Byzantine Emperor's personal guard, prostrate themselves before Christ in the Eastern form of homage and adoration known as *proskinesis*. Prophets stand below, expounding their sacred texts, and beneath them there is a charming Annunciation, where the Virgin drops her spindle in amazement as Gabriel appears before her. In the nave the Nativity faces the 'Dormition of the Virgin', an Eastern tradition which held that the Virgin did not die, but was put to sleep, and her soul taken from her body, in the form of a swaddled baby, by Christ. In the aisles near the entrance are two splendid mosaics of Roger II being crowned by Christ (as at Monreale a gesture of political independence), and George of Antioch prostrating himself before the Virgin. These mosaics, covering the walls and ceiling of this small church, are much closer and therefore more tangible than those in Monreale. Here one can imagine the Norman courtiers, with their bejewelled wives swathed in silks, celebrating the Eucharist through clouds of incense.

La Martorana is very popular with Palermitans, and is often used for weddings and christenings. This brings it to life, and I remember once admiring the mosaics alone with only a young couple, waiting patiently for an interview with their parish priest, for company. Their nervousness gave a sense of intimacy to the church which is so often lost in the grander settings of the great cathedrals of the island.

The second great Norman building outside Palermo is the cathedral at Cefalù. Perched on a headland overlooking the sea, with a great rock rising at its back, it dominates the fishing port at its feet. The drive along the coast, past fields of oranges, soon makes you forget the urban sprawl of Palermo. To savour the charm of Cefalù to the full, delay your visit to the cathedral until you have sampled the *fritto misto* or the *pesce spada alla griglia* (grilled swordfish) in one of the restaurants along the harbour front. (If your stomach can wait, you could dash up to the museum first to see Antonello da Messina's portrait of a man with sly, venal features which cynics equate,

La Martorana is one of the most intimate of the Norman churches of Sicily. You can experience the brilliant colouring of the mosaics at close quarters.

The cathedral of Cefalù stands in a commanding position overlooking the sea. The mosaic of Christ Pantocrator in the apse is one of the finest in existence.

Santo Spirito in Palermo is well off the tourist trail. This Norman church was the site of the Sicilian Vespers, one of the most dramatic moments in Sicilian history.

quite wrongly, with the typical Sicilian character.)

Monreale, like the Cappella Palatina, hints at the exoticism of the Norman kings, with their fluent knowledge of Arabic and Greek, their harems and their opulent palaces. The cathedral at Cefalù, on the other hand, sums up their iron determination, their energetic building of castles throughout the island, and the ruthless methods by which they stamped out all opposition – to the extent that, of the three hundred mosques which the Arabs had built in Palermo, not one remains.

Cefalù Cathedral, a rugged Romanesque structure, flanked by two towers, and set at the summit of a sloping piazza, looks as though it could withstand an earthquake. It was begun in 1131 to honour an oath made by the newly crowned Roger II, who had been shipwrecked off this coast. A consummate politician, Roger merely used the shipwreck as an excuse to erect a cathedral to proclaim his status and his independence from the Papacy. The result is a masterpiece of the Norman style, built over the succeeding century; the façade was added in 1240 by Giovanni Panettera.

The interior is a classic example of the problems of restoring an architectural palimpsest. The decision was taken in the 1970s to take out as much of the post-Norman decoration as possible. The result is impressively gaunt, with the exception of the baroque choir, but characteristic of the present fashion of zealously pursuing aesthetic purity, as though a building's history can be frozen at a particular moment.

However, nothing can detract from Cefalù's chief glory: the mosaic in the apse, whose glowing colours are ideally suited to emphasize Christ as Pantocrator, with the Virgin in prayer beneath, attended by Archangels, Apostles, saints and prophets. The Christ Pantocrator, executed in 1148, is one of the most solemn, monumental and majestic images of the Saviour in existence (but don't take too seriously the traditional theory that this is the actual likeness of Christ).

Cefalù is a good starting-point for an exploration of inland Sicily up towards the citadel of Enna, and this is especially rewarding in Easter week, when many of the most ancient festivals are enacted with a passion based on centuries of tradition. If, on the other hand, you are returning to Palermo, and have ever been stirred by the story of the Sicilian Vespers, or seen Verdi's rousing opera, you might like to visit the church of Santo Spirito. It is tucked away in a cemetery near the railway station, and can be reached by taking Via di Vespro, on the south side of Corso Tukory, which runs west of the station.

This simple Norman church was founded in 1177 by Walter Offamiglio (a comical Sicilian adaptation of Walter of the Mill), Archbishop of Palermo and regent to the young King William II, on a day of ill omen during an eclipse of the sun. It was here, on Easter Monday, 1282, that the first blow was struck against the hated Angevin soldiers (from the province of Anjou in France), as they jostled the Sicilian women about to celebrate vespers. As the bells of Palermo's churches summoned the faithful to prayer, the message spread like wildfire to massacre the Frenchmen. Within a week the whole island was ablaze, and even Messina was taken. Byzantine gold, the wily intrigues of John of Procida, and the intervention of Peter of Aragon, ensured that, for once, Sicilian courage was rewarded and the revolt successful. The fame of the Sicilian Vespers has never died, and Verdi's opera was a clarion call to nineteenth-century Italians to regain their nationhood and throw out the occupying Austrians.

When the Sicilians were searching for French suspects in 1282, the death sentence was passed on anyone who mispronounced the word *ciceri*, which is apparently impossible for a French speaker to say correctly – although hardly easy for anyone with a Sicilian knife at his throat. By an extraordinary quirk of fate, a friend of mine was lost recently in a back street in Palermo and, to his consternation, heard the locals pointing at him and muttering '*Ciceri*'. Such is the living power of Sicilian history.

Overleaf: The Virgin Annunciate, her hand raised in surprise, is seen through a forest of columns amidst the richness, beauty and mystery of the mosaics in the church of La Martorana in Palermo.

119

DECORUM AND DECADENCE

ORATORIO DI SANTA ZITA · ORATORIO DEL ROSARIO DI SAN DOMENICO
ORATORIO DI SAN LORENZO · VILLA PALAGONIA, BAGHERIA

Serpotta's carvings in the Oratorio di Santa Zita are a triumph of light-hearted rococo sculpture.

On 8 October 1571, in one of the decisive battles in history, the Christian fleet, consisting of contingents from Venice, Spain and the Papacy, crushed the mighty Turkish navy in the bay of Lepanto. To celebrate this famous victory, Pope Gregory XIII instituted the Festival of the Rosary in 1573. In this atmosphere of optimism and triumph, symptomatic of the resurgent forces of the Counter-Reformation, St Philip Neri founded the first of his oratories in Rome, a place where brethren could meet together to recite the Rosary and pray. These oratories were joyful affairs; they were highly decorated and filled with music, composed by St Philip's contemporary Palestrina, and were to provide a formative influence on theatre and opera. (If you want to infuriate your more intellectual friends, try asking them the derivation of the word oratorio.)

In the heart of Palermo, a city that once inspired countless travellers with its beauty but was badly damaged in the Second World War, stand three exquisite oratories, filled with the stucco sculptures of Giacomo Serpotta (1656-1732). A mixture of plaster, lime and marble dust, on an underlying framework of wood, wire and rags, stucco was favoured by the poorer religious orders because it was so cheap. Serpotta was one of the most able craftsmen in this fragile medium who has ever lived, and you can easily see his three greatest masterpieces in a couple of hours, leaving time either to enjoy the other sites in the centre of Palermo, or to visit the extravagantly decorated Villa Palagonia at Bagheria.

The most northerly of the three oratories, and much the best lit, is the Oratorio di Santa Zita, which commemorates the Battle of Lepanto. It stands on Via Valverde, which runs off Via Roma opposite the

main post office. You reach it by ascending a staircase which overlooks a small courtyard, passing a self-portrait of Serpotta, who gazes out with amused detachment. Serpotta worked here between 1685 and 1717, and the atmosphere of the oratory sums up the unashamedly light-hearted attitude to religion of the era. It is dedicated to the Rosary, but the bas-reliefs depicting the joyful and sorrowful mysteries of the Rosary pale beside the putti swarming over the walls in a riot of excitement. Between the reliefs, a series of seated allegorical women, the height of fashionable elegance in their panniered dresses, looks down at the spectator.

The *pièce de résistance* is the entrance wall, designed as a vast sculpted curtain on which the Virgin gives the Rosary to St Dominic, and looks down on the Battle of Lepanto. But once again the spectator's attention is diverted from the religious content by two worldly urchins seated beneath the battle among a pile of muskets, helmets and breastplates. The oratory is a favourite for Palermo society weddings, and you can almost visualize the arrival of Figaro and Susanna to the strains of Mozart's music.

Emerging from the oratory, head east down Via Valverde, and take the first right into Via Squarcialupo, which takes you to the Oratorio del Rosario di San Domenico (the precise instructions on the door on how to get in are, somewhat surprisingly for Sicily, entirely accurate). Before going in, notice the extraordinary house on the left of the entrance, which is squashed between the apse of the church of San Domenico and the oratory.

In this oratory, dedicated to the Rosary in 1578, a decade after the founding of the Order, Serpotta was

Starting-point: Oratorio di Santa Zita

Recommended time: Short day

Length of tour: 10 miles (16km)

Best time of year: Avoid mid-summer

Finishing-point: Villa Palagonia, Bagheria

The Oratorio del Rosario di San Domenico is decorated with baroque paintings and Serpotta's elegant statues of allegorical women.

obliged to fit his sculptures, executed in 1710-17, around the seventeenth-century paintings hanging in the chapel. The most famous of these, over the high altar, is Van Dyck's splendid 'Madonna of the Rosary', painted in Genoa in 1628 after the Fleming had wisely fled a virulent outbreak of the plague in Palermo.

The restrictions on Serpotta seem to have merely excited his fertile imagination. From the moment you enter the antechamber where putti scattered around the walls are fooling about with the symbols of the Passion, it is quite apparent that he is determined to impose his light-hearted view of religion. A measure of his success is the way that our attention is concentrated on the female figures posing between the dark and rather gloomy Caravaggesque canvases. In turn elegant, languid and provocative, these supple, coquettish ladies, in their jewels and lace, seem to have just alighted from their carriages on their way to a Spanish viceregal ball. Perhaps Serpotta rated Fortezza most highly, since he included his signature of a lizard (*sirpuzza* in Sicilian dialect – a pun on his name) on the column on which the shapely lady, with her elaborate head-dress, leans.

The Oratorio di San Lorenzo is hidden in a back street of Palermo. It provides an unlikely setting for Serpotta's inspired sculpture.

The third oratory, dedicated to San Lorenzo, was decorated by Serpotta in 1699-1707, immediately preceding his work at San Domenico. I particularly like its shabby, unpretentious charm. To reach it you need to cross the famous Vucciria market, a frenzied muddle of stalls, where the display of fish, fruit and vegetables is a real art form, the vivid reds, yellows and greens of the peppers and tomatoes contrasting with the purples and blacks of the aubergines. The king of the market stall is the swordfish, his razor-sharp blade pointing skywards. The richness of the sights, smells and sounds captures the flavour of an Oriental bazaar. I recently happened on the darker side of Sicilian life while passing through the market when I spotted two youths (scarcely justifying the Mafia title of 'Men of Honour'), in blue shirts and dark ties, helping themselves to whatever caught their fancy, with the stall-holders feverishly cursing them behind their backs.

On the south side of the market runs the Via Vittorio Emanuele. Just beyond lies the Piazza San Francesco, with the little Oratorio di San Lorenzo tucked away behind a wholly anonymous entrance off Via Immacolatella 5. The tragedy of this oratory is the loss of the Caravaggio of the Nativity which hung over the altar until it was stolen in 1969. Its absence at least meant that for many years there was no need to alter the building to improve security. Its approach through a dilapidated courtyard, and even the rather shabby state of the chapel itself, were almost miraculously preserved from the rapacious hands of the restoration industry. However, at the time of writing, the building was being restored and I sincerely hope that the lightness and elegance of Serpotta's stucco sculptures will be fully revealed without lessening the charm of this little chapel.

Of the three oratories, this is the most intimate, and, with its two organs in the choir, surrounded by figures playing a variety of instruments, the most suitable for the performance of an oratorio. One can imagine the music-loving Serpotta relaxing from his labours by playing the lute while up on the scaffolding.

The small scale of the interior focuses your attention on the extraordinary detail of the stuccoes. Perhaps because the scenes from the lives of St Lawrence and St Francis offered more scope for originality, the reliefs assume more importance, and are not completely dwarfed by the animated female figures, the swarming putti, and the *Ignudi* (naked figures), showing the influence of Annibale Carracci's ceiling in the Palazzo Farnese in Rome, and Michelangelo's Sistine ceiling. The strongest image is the central scene, on the wall facing the street, of St Lawrence being lowered on to his grill, angled in sharp perspective, while a Roman soldier on bended knee stokes the coals. Two of the most beautiful figures are the women in relief at the entrance to the choir, which hark back beyond baroque Rome to the great sculptors of Quattrocento Florence.

Despite its hideous surroundings, the Villa Palagonia, with its fantastic statues, is one of the most fascinating buildings of the eighteenth century. Its creator was, very probably, quite mad.

To the Anglo-Saxon mind, brought up to appreciate purity of decoration, an attractive feature of Serpotta's art is the whiteness of the stuccoes. This is most apparent in the Oratorio di Santa Zita and di San Lorenzo, although the Sicilian love of opulence is evident in some of the minor details, such as the seats inlaid with mother-of-pearl and supported by carved wooden figures, and the altar of San Lorenzo composed of lapis lazuli, gold, agate and porphyry.

You can now decide whether you would prefer to press on to Bagheria, or stay in Palermo. If you want to try one of the restaurants in the centre of the city, of which there is no shortage, you might like to sample one of the local pastas, such as *maccheroni con le sarde* (pasta tubes with sardines) or *annelletti alla Palermitana* (pasta rings with meat balls and tomato sauce), or *involtini* (meat slices rolled and stuffed), or one of any number of fish dishes.

If Serpotta's figures, with their refined elegance and provocative poses, come straight out of a rococo boudoir, the statues on the garden wall of the Villa Palagonia in Bagheria, which lies just east of Palermo along the coast, seem closer to an eighteenth-century Bacchanal. The exuberance of the musicians, the figures riding bizarre animals, many of them with human heads, and the violence of the animals fighting one another, reflect a truly primitive zest for life. The fertility of invention, and the variety of gestures and expressions, are matched by the fecundity of the garden, with its abundance of oranges, lemons, figs, and prickly pears, whose leaves resemble contorted hands stretching towards the sky.

The Prince of Palagonia, who commissioned these statues for his garden in the mid-eighteenth century, was a highly eccentric character whose taste would have delighted the surrealists. He was a magpie in his collecting, mixing heaps of coloured glass with mounds of porcelain, furniture, clocks, and all sorts of reptiles, spiders and scorpions.

The villa in which he housed his collection was built for his grandfather by Tomaso Mario Napoli in 1705-15, and reflects the prevalent late baroque style in its curved façades, the complexity of its staircase, and the ornate fantasy of the decoration of the door, the window frames and the coat of arms over the main entrance. The Villa Palagonia is the most interesting of the numerous villas which made Bagheria the most fashionable environ of Palermo in the eighteenth century. Sadly, the urban sprawl of the modern city has almost totally overrun the surrounding lemon groves to which the nobility used to drive when indulging in romantic liaisons.

The decoration of the villa reflects the eclectic nature of the Prince's collection. Just as the statues in the garden combine an abundance of different elements, with beggars, dwarves and figures from the *commedia dell' arte* jostling with the gods and goddesses of antiquity, so the interior blends the rococo and neoclassical styles. The oval entry hall, dominated by *trompe-l'oeil* frescoes of the labours of Hercules, leads into the fantasy of the ballroom, where coloured marble busts of the Prince's ancestors gesture from their niches beneath a shimmering glass ceiling. A fictive balustrade surmounted by urns and birds, and interspersed with rococo mirrors, increases the illusion that we are gazing up into the sky. The side rooms are more restrained, with the heads of classical writers and philosophers set within roundels. The chapel, which was the most extraordinary room of all, has long since disappeared, sparing us the sight of a marble bust of a woman being eaten by centipedes and scorpions, and the figure of St Francis hanging by the neck, with illuminated hands and feet.

The villa has always produced strong reactions in the spectator. Goethe was repelled by its atmosphere of decadence, but others were inspired by its startling originality – none more so than Sir John Soane who came here on his Grand Tour in 1778. The shallow dome of the morning room of Soane's house in Lincoln's Inn Fields, London, decorated with pieces of glass, has a similarly inventive quality, if slightly less surreal than the ballroom of the Villa Palagonia.

THE LEGACY OF GREECE

SEGESTA · ROCCHE DI CUSA · SELINUNTE · AGRIGENTO

The site of Segesta is one of the most romantic in Europe. The unfinished Doric temple stands alone among the vines and olives.

Fifth-century Greek art represents one of the summits of human achievement. The age of Pericles and Phidias inspired all that we most admire in classical art and literature, and, in turn, the art of the Renaissance. The Greek world stretched far beyond the confines of Greece herself, and one of the most rewarding places in which to gain a real understanding of the beauty of her art and architecture is Sicily, which once vied with Athens herself as the standard-bearer of Greek culture. Indeed, at the climax of the Peloponnesian War in 415BC, it was Syracuse, with its vast resources, which emerged victorious over the great Athenian invading force.

Sicily was an immensely rich island in antiquity, far richer than Greece herself. The island was seldom at peace, for the Greeks squabbled incessantly, and when they were not feuding amongst themselves, they were fighting the Carthaginians, who had colonized the west coast. There were manifold attractions for both races: fertile land, ideal for agriculture, secure harbours, quarryable stone, trees for fuel and boat-building, and hills providing pasture for goats. The Greeks introduced the vine and the olive, both of which flourished, and, with their new-found wealth, erected a series of magnificent temples, using the slave labour of their enemies captured in battle. Their great victory over the Carthaginians at the Battle of Himera in 480BC, supposedly on the same day that the Athenians annihilated the Persian navy in the bay of Salamis, encouraged a building boom, including many of the finest Greek temples ever constructed.

In a long day's sightseeing, you can visit the finest surviving temples on the island. They look their best in spring, when they are surrounded by wild flowers, which grow in profusion throughout Sicily. If you are coming from Palermo, you would be

well advised to begin with Segesta. The drive west along the coast on the A29 *autostrada* is very impressive, as you pass beneath the jagged peaks of the mountains where the bandit Giuliano reigned supreme in the late 1940s. Beyond Partinico the country opens out, and Segesta stands in the folds of the hills which stretch to Trapani passing Calatafimi, where Garibaldi and the Thousand won a famous victory on 15 May 1860, on the epic march from Marsala to Palermo.

Segesta is one of the most romantic of all classical sites, although locals tell me that it was even more so when you were obliged to reach it by donkey and cart. The simple Doric temple, unfinished and bare of ornament, has remained unaltered since the day it was built. The incomplete capitals, the lack of fluting and bases to the columns, and the absence of a roof, help to give it a much stronger atmosphere than many more polished Greek buildings. The tinkling of sheep and goat bells, the chirping of the finches who live in the entablature, and the giant fennel which so impressed Goethe on his visit in 1786, have remained unchanged for millennia. Even if you are unlucky enough to encounter a horde of tourists, you can always escape into the seclusion of the pine wood standing behind the temple.

The history of the temple is most unusual. Originally founded by the Elymnians, Segesta became a relatively small outpost, precariously situated between Carthaginian settlements, which dominated this part of the island, and the aggressive Greek cities of the southern coast. Her bitterest rival was Selinunte, with whom Segesta was in conflict throughout the sixth and fifth centuries BC. Consequently, in 426BC, she sought help from Athens, then at the height of her power. In order to impress

Starting-point: Palermo
Recommended time: Very full day or a day and a half
Length of tour: 112 miles (180km)
Best time of year: April for the wild flowers, or October/November
Finishing-point: Agrigento

the Athenians, the Segestans immediately began work on their temple, whose exterior was virtually complete when the delegation arrived in 416BC. The Athenians were royally entertained on gold plate which had been borrowed from the locals, and so impressed were they, that they were persuaded to join their hosts in an alliance, and to launch their ill-fated expedition against Syracuse.

To my mind the rugged beauty of this temple (still surrounded by vines and olives), designed by a Greek architect for a people living on the fringes of the Greek world, is the best evocation of the extraordinary, far-flung achievement of their civilization.

An integral, but peripheral part of the Greek world, Segesta had its moment of glory when it changed allegiance from Athens to Carthage, and engineered the destruction of Selinunte in 409BC. The town continued to flourish in the fourth century BC, but was increasingly threatened by the covetous tyrants of Syracuse and was eventually taken and razed by Agathocles in 307BC. The Carthaginians retook Segesta, but the inhabitants, ever mindful of the main chance, soon put themselves under the suzerainty of Rome. In a new era of prosperity, the Segestans built a theatre in a commanding position on top of the hill, which offers views down to the Gulf of Castellamare. The city was finally destroyed by the Saracens, leaving it to the Romantics to rediscover the temple which so perfectly fitted their idea of the sublime.

The temples of Selinunte, mostly destroyed, possess a primitive grandeur. Huge fragments of columns lie amid the undergrowth. The Acropolis overlooks the sea.

The quarry of Rocche di Cusa, used by the builders of Selinunte, is very evocative of the world of ancient Greece and is well off the tourist trail.

If you have a vivid imagination, and are allergic to the threat of large groups, you can be sure of finding peace and quiet at the remote site of Rocche di Cusa, which lies on the south coast near Selinunte. You reach it by taking the *autostrada* beyond Castelvetrano towards Mazara del Vallo, turning off to Campobello, and following the yellow signs heading south to Scavi and Rocche di Cusa.

This is the ancient quarry for the temples of Selinunte. In a setting of wild flowers, olives and almond trees, blocks of stone, some of truly immense proportions, lie scattered throughout the site. Some of the stones still bear the rope marks and the scarred rock face hacked away by the slaves toiling in the fierce heat of the sun. But do not let your imagination get too carried away; snakes enjoy untended classical sites every bit as much as we do. A visit to Rocche di Cusa helps to put into perspective the vast size of the temples at Selinunte, which lies 13km to the east along a pretty road through olive groves, interspersed by stands of eucalyptus.

Selinunte possesses no single building as complete as those at Segesta and Agrigento, but the size of the archaeological area, untouched by the ravages of modern development, enables you to experience, better than anywhere else in Sicily, the scale of an ancient Greek city. Founded by the inhabitants of Syracuse in 680BC, and named after the wild celery that still grows on the site, Selinunte flourished throughout the fifth century until it was brutally sacked by the Carthaginians, in alliance with Segesta, and its inhabitants were massacred or sold into slavery. The savagery of its destruction was followed by numerous earthquakes which meant that the site was completely buried for centuries. It was rediscovered in the sixteenth century, and excavated by William Harris and Samuel Angell in 1822-3. The metopes (sculpted reliefs) that they dug up are now the chief glory of the Archaeological Museum in Palermo.

The archaeological site of Selinunte divides into two parts: the Acropolis, dedicated to the gods of Olympus, overlooking the sea, and the eastern plateau. The latter is the more impressive and includes the remains of three great temples. The first of these, known prosaically as Temple E, has largely been re-erected, and dominates the skyline. It dates from Selinunte's heyday in the fifth century BC and is built of the golden limestone which is such an attractive feature of Sicilian architecture.

Beyond it lie the ruinous Temples F and G,

Opposite: The classical purity of the Temple of Castor and Pollux seen at Agrigento. Right: The rugged beauty of the temple at Segesta, perhaps the most evocative of all Greek temples in Sicily, represents the end of the classic period of Greek architecture.

whose fallen columns and entablatures appear as though they had just crashed to the ground. Temple G, the largest of the three, is wonderfully evocative of the fallen grandeur of antiquity, and is covered in wild flowers and figs growing among the tumbled columns. From here Temple E stands out against the bright blue of the sea and sky. The Acropolis, towards the sea, with its temple and lines of streets and houses, covers an even larger area, but is less atmospheric than the temples to the east.

The temples of Agrigento are the most complete ancient Greek monuments in Sicily. The exquisite beauty of the Temple of Concord rivals the Parthenon itself.

The third of the great Greek sites in Sicily is Agrigento, which lies on the coast some 95km east of Selinunte on the SS115. A visit to the site requires a little more planning, because it stands on a ridge overlooking the hideous modern town. By far the best way to approach the temples is from the Hotel Villa Athena. If you are not fortunate enough to be staying in the hotel (which has the added bonus of allowing you to visit the temples at night), park your car at the far end of the hotel car-park, turn right, and follow the path across the stream and up through the olive and almond grove to the Temple of Concord.

From this angle, particularly in the early morning, when the sun is shining full on the golden limestone of the east façade, and the blue of the sky is visible between the Doric columns, the perfect proportions of the temple make an unforgettable impact. It seems miraculous that the temple has survived so perfectly, and this is due to its transformation into a Christian church in the sixth century by the quaintly named St Gregory of the Turnips (San Gregorio delle Rape). The walls and arches in the interior date from this period but, mercifully, the exterior has remained untouched.

The Temple of Concord dates from c.430BC, when Agrigento (or Akragas, as the Greeks named it), was at the height of its power. Originally founded in 581BC by the inhabitants of Rhodes and Gela, Agrigento quickly grew in size. The tyrant Theron, who played a crucial part in the Battle of Himera, began a programme of building, using slaves as free labour, for which the Carthaginians exacted a terrible revenge when they sacked Agrigento in 406BC.

The Temple of Hera stands to the east of the Temple of Concord at the end of a road, flanked by Byzantine rock tombs on one side, and on the other by a profusion of nature: olives, almonds, figs, carobs and euphorbia. It was erected in 470BC, and twenty-five columns still stand in a dominant position at the summit of the ridge. Back in the 1770s, Henry Swinburne, one of the first Grand Tourists to visit the temples of Sicily, wrote: 'The view of the temple and the delicious orchards that surround it are indeed precious to landscape painters.' It is easy to see why.

The most atmospheric view of the temple is from the road on the southern side of the site, where it perches above the fissured rock face, the soil long since eroded, resembling the prints of gigantic elephants' feet. Immediately below the temple, vast chunks of rock, overthrown by an earthquake, dot the hillside, one of them crushing an olive tree. From this viewpoint the works of man seem puny compared with the primeval forces of nature.

Returning to the Temple of Concord, continue down the hill past a sea of red sainfoin to the Temple of Herakles by the main entrance. This temple dates from the late sixth century BC, and has been devastated by earthquakes. One of the multitude of charges that Cicero laid at the door of the corrupt Roman Governor Verres was that he had tried to steal a famous statue of Herakles from the temple.

The largest of all the temples lies across the main road. The gigantic Temple of Olympian Zeus, over 100 metres long and 50 metres wide, was begun after the Battle of Himera. Although left unfinished when Agrigento fell in 406BC, and despite being devastated by earthquakes and pilfered for its stone, it remains a testament to the ambitions of the city. An 8-metre high Gigante, which once stood between the Doric columns to support the entablature, lies among the ruins, as though it, like Samson, had brought the whole edifice crashing down. The rope marks cut into the stone, and the olives and wild flowers growing among the broken columns, capture an atmosphere of fallen glory.

The last of the temples, the Temple of Castor and Pollux, stands on the edge of a hidden valley filled with orange trees and birdsong, a far cry from the gruesome apartment blocks that have so disfigured modern Agrigento. The scope and variety of the temples make this the most important classical site in Sicily, and show how the enterprising Greek colonists rivalled the achievements of their motherland.

BAROQUE EXTRAVAGANCE

NOTO · MODICA · RAGUSA IBLA

Noto is a perfectly preserved small baroque town, built in a mellow honey-coloured stone. The main buildings were designed by Rosario Gagliardi.

To the Anglo-Saxon, weaned on a diet of Gothic churches and Georgian country houses, there remains something deeply suspect about the baroque. How can the effect of any style depend so much on its purely emotional appeal? This attitude is so ingrained that it is almost impossible to overcome. The answer is to try Noto, perhaps the most instantly appealing of all baroque towns, although, at the time of writing, many of its finest buildings are under scaffolding. For the instant convert, the name to conjure with is Rosario Gagliardi, an architect of genius whose work rivals in its dramatic effect that of Bernini and Borromini. In a day out from Syracuse you can take in Noto and Gagliardi's baroque churches in the towns of Modica and Ragusa.

The town of Noto, standing some 30km southeast of Syracuse on the SS115, possesses great advantages for the sightseer. It can easily be seen on foot in a couple of hours, with little risk of being run down, robbed or molested; it is a town of striking façades (always easier to appreciate for their picturesque qualities than interiors); and it is entirely constructed out of porous limestone which has mellowed to a beautiful honey colour. In contrast, Catania, a grander baroque city of the same date, full of traffic and people, is built in a dull, black lava. Consequently few people, least of all dubious northerners, visit it, although they would doubtless fail to see the irony in their emotional response to what is, essentially, an emotional style of architecture.

Noto Antica, a small, provincial town on the periphery of the vast Spanish Empire, was devastated by an earthquake in 1693. So catastrophic was this upheaval that a drastic decision was taken in order to prevent such an event happening again: eight of the forty damaged towns were to be moved to new sites.

A commission was set up under the Duke of Camastra, and the King of Spain took a personal interest in the planning of the new towns. They were to have wide streets and low palaces to try to minimize the impact of another calamity.

The actual site of Noto, on a slope some 7km from Noto Antica, was determined by the priorities of defence, especially against pirates, the availability of water, and the proximity of agricultural land. The plan, interestingly enough, looks back beyond the baroque, to the ideas of Scamozzi, a pupil of Palladio. The town's people must have been a religious lot or, more probably, the church must have been extremely rich and powerful, since 32 churches were erected for a population of ten thousand, the three finest in the plum positions overlooking the main squares. A referendum was held in 1698 to determine the popularity of the move. The clergy and nobility voted in favour of the new site, whereas the middle classes, grumbling about the loss of trade, voted against. A clear majority voted to return to the old site but, in true Sicilian fashion, their wishes were ignored.

At the heart of Noto the Corso Vittorio Emanuele and the Via Cavour run in parallel, following the contours of the hill. The two streets are filled with a series of magnificent palaces and churches erected in the eighteenth century by Rosario Gagliardi and his pupil Vincenzo Sinatra (now the most famous of all Sicilian names, thanks to Hollywood). The town's importance has earned it the status of a UNESCO site (whatever that means), although it still suffers the same problems as anywhere else in Sicily: a splendid show of snapdragons growing out of every façade, many of the best buildings smothered in scaffolding, and interiors seemingly for ever *in restauro*.

The best way to take in the town is to wander at

Starting-point: Noto

Recommended time: Full day

Length of tour: 33 miles (53km)

Best time of year: April/May or September/October

Finishing-point: Ragusa Ibla

Opposite: Gagliardi's two churches in Ragusa are triumphs of baroque vitality and movement. The façade of San Giorgio, with its long flight of steps, soars above the piazza. Left: The interior of San Giuseppe displays a true lightness and delicacy of decoration.

leisure. Many of the churches show the influence of the Roman baroque. The most imposing and theatrical is Gagliardi's San Domenico (1703-27), in Piazza XVI Maggio, with columns protruding from a convex façade to emphasize the play of light and shade. Gagliardi paid great attention to the details such as the shell niches and honeycombs, and the dogs seated on the volutes (a pun on the Dominicans, also known as *domini canes* – dogs of the lord). The Duomo in the Piazza Municipio is a simpler building, designed to be seen up a steep flight of steps, where the skyline of the façade can be admired to maximum effect. The central section, balanced by two bell towers, looks back to Sant' Agnese in the Piazza Navona in Rome.

Many of the palaces have fanciful, curved balconies. The most imaginative are those designed by Gagliardi for the Palazzo Nicolaci Villadorata in Via Corrado Nicolaci, flanking the Duomo, where grimacing lions, mermaids, prancing horses, grotesque faces and mythological figures form elaborate wall brackets supporting balconies with characteristic convex iron railings.

The grandeur of the plan of Noto, and the spaciousness of the streets, disguise the fact that it is really a provincial Sicilian town. You can see this clearly if you walk along Via Cavour. The palaces and churches on either side create the effect of decayed magnificence, but the side streets running up the hill could be found in any small town on the island, with old women sitting on their doorsteps exchanging gossip, children practising wheelies on their bicycles, and washing strung out on a line between a church façade and a lamp-post.

Gagliardi's churches of San Giorgio in Modica and Ragusa Ibla stand in commanding positions at the head of long flights of steps.

Modica and Ragusa, some 40km further east, have escaped the surfeit of scaffolding that afflicts Noto. The sites of the two towns, standing at the summit of a spur and a ridge respectively, offered Gagliardi perfect opportunities to display his dramatic architectural gifts to the full. The church of San Giorgio in Modica, rebuilt following the disastrous earthquake of 1693, stands at the head of a dramatic flight of steps that rises from the lower part of the town. Gagliardi continues these sweeping curves in the façade of the church, which, with its vertical clusters of columns, provides a dynamic sense of movement.

The town of Ragusa Ibla, to the east beyond Modica, is equally spectacular, lying along a ridge and connected to the newer town by an even longer and steeper staircase. Once again Gagliardi's church of San Giorgio is placed in a wonderfully theatrical setting, at the top of a sloping piazza dominating the skyline. He introduced his favourite themes to the façade: protruding columns to accentuate the play of light and shade, and curved volutes and equestrian statues on rearing horses to enhance the effect of movement. The church looks very impressive, and the statues and flaming urns on the summit of the façade are particularly striking, when seen from across the gorge leading into the town.

The piazza facing San Giorgio is full of interest. All the houses have handsome ornate iron balconies, covered in flowers and washing. The Circolo di Conversazione (a Club) at the foot of the square is a fine, neoclassical building with Greek Doric pilasters, sphinxes and other classical motifs. Beside it, rows of old men pass the time of day seated on chairs in the street, watching the world go by. In the piazza below, the façade of the church of San Giuseppe, attributed to Gagliardi, is a simpler version of San Giorgio. The elliptical interior is in a light, rococo style, decorated with curly arabesque patterns and exotic grills to hide the nuns at their devotions.

The south-eastern corner of the island, so often overlooked by tourists, possesses an ancient landscape filled with tombs cut from the rock, troglodyte houses and other prehistoric dwellings. The ubiquitous prickly pears line the roadside, with cattle grazing beyond. The fields are separated by drystone walls, reminding one of rural Ireland or the Hebrides. In this provincial backwater it seems all the more surprising to find three towns with some of the finest baroque architecture in Europe.

TOUR 21

THE LAND OF THE LEOPARD

PIAZZA ARMERINA · CALTAGIRONE · SYRACUSE

The Villa Casale, just outside Piazza Armerina, contains some of the finest mosaics to have survived from antiquity. They include such startlingly modern features as women wearing bikinis.

Starting-point: Agrigento
Recommended time: Very full day or a day and a half
Length of tour: 155 miles (250km)
Best time of year: April/May or September/October
Finishing-point: Syracuse

It is all too easy to visit Sicily and see nothing of the interior of the island apart from the constricted view one gets from the *autostrada*. To do so is to miss an excellent opportunity to enjoy some of the grandest landscape in Europe. You can gain a good idea of the variety of the Sicilian countryside in a day's drive from Agrigento to Syracuse, taking in the splendours of the Roman mosaics at Piazza Armerina en route.

It is only when you have climbed from the coast towards Piazza Armerina that you begin to enjoy vistas over the ranges of hills unfolding in every direction. To the north-east you can catch tantalizing glimpses of Etna in the distance, with its characteristic plume of smoke. Further inland, the hill-town of Enna, with its famous belvedere, appears on the crest of a ridge. The landscape is bare and depopulated, with only the occasional building standing among fields of corn which stretch to the distant horizon. Little has changed since these wheat fields earned Sicily its reputation as the granary of the Roman Empire.

Piazza Armerina itself is one of the myriad hill-towns scattered throughout the interior of the island. Its baroque architecture, as so often in provincial Sicily, shows the strong influence of Spain, which ruled the island from the fourteenth to the eighteenth century. The Duomo, which dominates the skyline, is typical in this respect, showing a strong contrast in the façade between the ornate decoration of the doorway, with its barley-sugar columns, and the blank expanse of the surrounding wall. The interior, richly decorated in a blue and white colour scheme, contains a Crucifix attributed, rather ambitiously, to Antonello da Messina. The town is filled with the handsome façades of numerous churches and palaces, showing its importance as a provincial capital from the time of the Norman kings onwards. However, its chief glory is the Roman Villa Casale, which lies 5km to the south-west, in a setting of cypresses and pines.

The villa was known of in the eighteenth and nineteenth centuries, but systematic excavations did not begin until 1929, and the full extent of the mosaics was only unveiled in 1950. Its size, and the splendour of its mosaics, persuaded many scholars that it belonged to Maximian, the co-Emperor of Diocletian, in the late third century AD, but it now appears that it was the country residence of one of the wealthy owners of vast land holdings on the island. You enter the villa past the ancient aqueduct ('which directly supplied the fools of the thermal complex', in the somewhat bizarre words of the local guidebook). The approach is less than atmospheric: a gaudy pink roof to protect the mosaics, and some hideous municipal plants to provide colour co-ordination.

The interior, however, is quite extraordinary. You are suddenly conveyed into the hedonistic world of late antiquity. The mosaics celebrate the cultured taste of the owner and his guests: mythological scenes are interspersed with chariot races, fishing and hunting expeditions, and some sexual dalliance as light relief. The mosaics are so realistic that you can experience the emotion of the chariot race in the Circus Maximus in Rome, enjoy the excitement of the cupids as they land their catch and sport with dolphins, and share the drama of the hunt as the horsemen drive a herd of stags into a net, and a huntsman spears a boar as his wounded comrade lies helpless on the ground.

The mosaics cover the floors of the rooms around a peristyle court, and can be viewed from ramps

Left: Dawn light catches the
sea front on the island of
Ortygia in Syracuse.
Opposite: A view of Vizzini,
one of numerous unspoilt
hill-towns in the
mountainous interior
of Sicily.

above. On the far side is the great hunting corridor, a complex mosaic beginning with hunting scenes in Africa, and continuing with a fascinating depiction of the capture and transport by ship of the animals to Rome, where they were slaughtered in their thousands in the Colosseum. The artists, both here and in the other mosaics, seem to have possessed a natural ability in portraying animals, whether it is a hare crouching in a thicket, a bull struggling violently against his captors, or a tigress protecting her cubs. One of the most charming scenes is Orpheus playing to the animals: the fox, the lion, the hippo, the bear, the eagle and the pheasant, all of whom watch entranced.

Next to this scene is the famous mosaic of girls in bikinis indulging in various athletic contests. The artistic quality is inferior to that of the hunting scenes, but the women appear startlingly modern, as though they had just stepped out of a painting by Matisse. The owner's private quarters, at the highest point of the villa, depict a more sensual and light-hearted theme, as women, cupids, mermaids, and an exotic collection of animals and fish indulge in an aquatic Bacchanal. Next door, a fight between Pan and Eros introduces the theme of love. The idea of a building devoted to pleasure was taken up again by Agostino Chigi, with the help of his friend Raphael, in his sixteenth-century Villa Farnesina in Rome.

From Piazza Armerina, the road continues across an open landscape of corn fields, with a smattering of olives and fruit trees, to Caltagirone, the home of a flourishing ceramics industry. This is a quirky town, an unlikely place to find a high quality painting of the Trinity, supposedly by Roger van der Weyden, tucked away over a side altar in the church of San Giorgio, as well as a multitude of grandiose baroque façades, campanili covered in brightly coloured enamelled terracottas, and a soaring flight of steps which is lit up by tapestries of fire on the evening of local festivals.

From Caltagirone you pass through the dramatic scenery of the Iblean hills before descending to the coast. The small hill-town of Vizzini, with its umbrella pine and iron belfry silhouetted against the sky, sums up the charm of the interior, which has been spared the unsightly developments that disfigure the coastline. Beyond Vizzini the landscape loses its interest as it passes through a featureless terrain where cattle browse, before descending through a succession of orange and lemon groves to Syracuse.

Syracuse is very much a curate's egg of a city. The ancient capital of the Greeks, and the largest and most important city in Sicily until the Arabs transferred the capital to Palermo, it has lost much of its character due to modern development in the wake of widespread damage in the last war. Nevertheless, the archaeological area and the island of Ortygia remain two of the most attractive sites in Sicily.

The city of Syracuse was founded by Corinth in 734BC, and soon became the leading Greek city in Sicily. A succession of able tyrants defeated their Carthaginian rivals and embellished the city so magnificently that it rivalled Athens herself in beauty. It seemed that Syracuse was invincible. The Athenians were defeated in a massive attack in 415-13BC, as were the Carthaginians later, and it was not until 212BC, during the Second Punic War, that the Romans captured the city in spite of the Herculean efforts of the inhabitants, led by Archimedes, to defeat them. Thereafter Rome did her worst, stripping the city of her artistic possessions.

Despite Syracuse's hegemony among the Greek states in Sicily, her classical monuments, in the Archaeological Area enclosed in a public park, are much less intact than those of Segesta, Selinunte and Agrigento, although the classical atmosphere is much stronger. Little remains of the immense second-century altar, erected by the tyrant Hieron II for the sacrifice of four hundred bulls as part of Syracuse's victory celebrations at the end of the First Punic War. Beyond the altar, which lies to the left of the main entrance to the park is the Greek Theatre, carved out of the hillside, which is best visited during a performance of the Greek classics, when it really comes to life. The tyrants who ruled the city were anxious to stress their love of culture, and commissioned numerous plays, including Aeschylus's *The Persians* and *The Women of Etna*. In the second century BC, under the influence of the Romans, the standard of culture dropped, and the theatre was used for gladiatorial combats and *naumachiae* (naval combats on a flooded stage).

The most moving part of the site is the cave known as the Latomia del Paradiso, a cruel misnomer, since this is where, after the surrender of the Athenians in 413, the wretched prisoners were put to

The campanili of Caltagirone are covered in brightly coloured enamelled terracottas.

The island of Ortygia is much the most attractive part of Syracuse. The only part of the mainland city worth visiting is the Archaeological Area, with the Greek theatre.

work deep within the bowels of the rock – a setting reminiscent, in its claustrophobic quality, of a Piranesi etching. This impression is enhanced by the marks, still visible, of the Athenian slaves' efforts to hack the stone from the rock face. These were the prisoners who had successfully recited passages of Euripides' *Elektra* to their captors. All those who failed, according to Plutarch, were immediately put to death. This savage mixture of culture and cruelty is characteristic of the Sicilian Greeks. One trembles to think how we would fare if put to the same test with the works of Shakespeare.

The cave was named by Caravaggio 'Dionysius's Ear', on account of the curious shape of its entrance, and because of its peculiar acoustic properties. Any sound is amplified, and according to legend, this enabled the tyrant Dionysius to listen from above to the conversation of the prisoners. The Latomia is surrounded by a semi-tropical garden where magnolia grandiflora, palms, figs, mulberries and pittosporum flourish.

The rest of mainland Syracuse is a disappointment, and you would be well advised to head straight for the island of Ortygia, where you can escape from the worst of the traffic. Driving in Syracuse has rules all of its own, and probably comes closest to the chaos of Naples. Most writers cite the exuberance of the people as evidence of their freedom from the Mafia, whose traditional power base is the west of the island, but it seems more probable that the confusion, bordering on anarchy, in which the Syracusans choose to live is a product of their Greek ancestry, and that this also accounts for their greater similarity to the Neapolitans. The Syracusans are seen at their best on a summer's evening at the Greek Theatre, when the whole audience, including even the youngest children, sit entranced.

Ortygia is a town in its own right, and has retained its narrow streets which effectively shut out the traffic. The long vistas up these streets, between wrought-iron balconies laden with geraniums, encapsulate its charm. There is a naturalness to life here

– as when a couple embrace on the back of a motorbike, an upturned bath is propped up against a Palladian arch, or a piece of scaffolding is used as an impromptu washing line – which is very appealing. This means that there is never a dull moment, even if you have just discovered, as is all too likely, that the Galleria Regionale in Palazzo Bellomo, in Via Capodieci, is closed indefinitely. If the museum is open, you can enjoy a damaged Annunciation by Antonello da Messina, and Caravaggio's highly charged 'Burial of St Lucy', a late work of 1608 in which the figures are enveloped in the surrounding darkness.

The buildings on the island are never regarded purely as monuments, and the most important palaces stage concerts during the summer season. This applies even to the extraordinary Duomo, where the Greek columns of the original fifth-century Temple of Athena have been incorporated into the side walls. The corrupt Roman Governor Verres (see page 130), had a field day in Syracuse, stripping the inner walls of the temple of the famous ivory panels erected by the Syracusan tyrant Agathocles to celebrate one of his victories. Verres was not alone in his avarice, and centuries of looting have left the interior almost completely bare, apart from the high baroque chapel of St Lucy.

Beside the Duomo in the attractive curved piazza stands the baroque Municipio. Opposite is the beautiful façade of the Palazzo Beneventano del Bosco built between 1778 and 1788 by the local architect Luciano Ali.

The Duomo is constantly used for weddings, christenings or services of thanksgiving for the safe return of the body of St Lucy, the patron saint of Syracuse, which was stolen in 1990. Even during the most solemn service, some of the participants are to be seen gossiping in the portico beneath the splendid high baroque façade. One of my favourite vignettes was the sight of a bridegroom processing up the nave on the arm of his mother. Such are the varieties of experience you are likely to encounter in Sicily.

INDEX